PEE WEES

PEE WEES

CONFESSIONS OF A HOCKEY PARENT

RICH COHEN

Farrar, Straus and Giroux

New York

Farrar, Straus and Giroux
120 Broadway, New York 10271

Grateful acknowledgment is made to Jeremy Medoff for permission
to reproduce the photographs on pages ii–iii, 4, 79, 126, 153,
192, and 209, and to *Can/Am* magazine for permission
to reproduce the image on page 162.
Photographs on pages 30, 35, 64, and 160 are from the
personal collection of the author.

Library of Congress Cataloging-in-Publication Data
Names: Cohen, Rich, author.
Title: Pee wees : confessions of a hockey parent / Rich Cohen.
Description: First edition. | New York : Farrar, Straus and
Giroux, 2021.
Identifiers: LCCN 2020039384 | ISBN 9780374268015
(hardcover)
Subjects: LCSH: Hockey for children—Connecticut. |
Hockey—Social aspects—Connecticut. | Competition
(Psychology)—Social aspects. | Parent and child. | Cohen, Rich.
Classification: LCC GV848.6.C45 C65 2021 | DDC
796.962083—dc23
LC record available at https://lccn.loc.gov/2020039384

Our books may be purchased in bulk for promotional, educational,
or business use. Please contact your local bookseller or the
Macmillan Corporate and Premium Sales Department at
1-800-221-7945, extension 5442, or by email at
MacmillanSpecialMarkets@macmillan.com.

www.fsgbooks.com
www.twitter.com/fsgbooks • www.facebook.com/fsgbooks

1   3   5   7   9   10   8   6   4   2

If I were not to dedicate this book, and, what's more,

this entire hockey endeavor, with its early mornings,

ramshackle rinks, frozen weekends, road travel, injuries,

freak-outs, panics, pleasures, moments of self-love and

self-loathing, to my wife, Jessica, who led me through it

as a guide leads a wayfarer through an acid trip, there'd

be something seriously wrong with me.

So . . .

To Jessica, with love.

Hell is other hockey parents.

—JEAN-PAUL SARTRE, French philosopher

The secret of life is caring, but not that much.

—HERB COHEN, Brooklyn negotiator

Contents

2018–2019 Roster, Pee Wee A Ridgefield Bears

Head Coach: Pete Wilson

Parent-Coach: Alan Hendrix   Parent-Coach: Ralph Rizzo

Scheduler: Alan Hendrix   Manager: Terry Stanley

NO.	PLAYER	POSITION	AGE	HT.	WT.	FAV. NHL PLAYER	PARENTS
00	Dan Arcus	Goalie	12	5'6"	135 lb.	Henrik Lundqvist	Jocko & Camille
03	Jean Camus	Right Wing	11	5'2"	105 lb.	Guy Charron	Simone
04	Tommy McDermott	Center	12	4'8"	83 lb.	Brad Marchand	Bobby & Eunice
12	Rick Stanley	Defense	12	5'6"	135 lb.	Gordie Howe	Terry & Samantha
14	Joey McDermott	Left Wing	12	4'8"	81 lb.	Artemi Panarin	Bobby & Eunice
15	Duffy Taylor	Left Wing	11	4'10"	96 lb.	Mark Messier	Parky & Jill
19	Brian Rizzo	Defense	11	4'10"	98 lb.	Patrick Kane	Ralph & Sharon
32	Patrick Campi	Wing/Defense	12	5'6"	120 lb.	John Tavares	Gordon & Sue
33	Becky Goodman	Defense	12	5'7"	110 lb.	Hilary Knight	Bill & Roz
45	Micah Cohen	Left Wing	11	4'8"	81 lb.	Patrick Kane	Rich & Jessica
55	"Broadway Julie" Sherman	Right Wing	12	5'5"	103 lb.	Hilary Knight	Jerry & Geri
64	Barry Meese	Center	12	5'2"	103 lb.	Connor McDavid	Judd & Gail
65	Leo Moriarty	Right Wing	11	5'1"	99 lb.	Zach Hyman	Albert
66	"Broadway Jenny" Hendrix	Center/Wing	12	4'7"	77 lb.	Kendall Coyne	Alan & Grace
89	Roman Holian	Right Wing	11	5'3"	107 lb.	Max Pacioretty	Rob & Victoria

Author's Note

What follows is the story of a single season in the life of a youth hockey team, the Pee Wee A Bears of Ridgefield, Connecticut, consisting of fifteen eleven- and twelve-year-old boys and girls. In its intensities, the story of this season, which I have translated from life, mirrors the ups and downs experienced by every American parent. It can be football. It can be dance, fencing, baseball, basketball, soccer, theater, or lacrosse. Here it happens to be hockey, where, in the course of eight months, from August to April, my son and I experienced the highest highs and lowest lows of our lives together. When, in the spring of 2019, I asked my big sister why I cared so much, why I was losing my mind, she said, "This is what it's like to send your kids into the world. Your child is not just like you or raised by you—he *is* you. And when something wrong or unfair happens to him, it brings up things that are so deep and primal it feels like you will die from it."

Names of people, teams, and places have been changed, ditto dates and details.

PEE WEES

APRIL

Every kind of car in the parking lot. German cars. Italian cars. Jeeps with the tops down. Inside the rink, the parents, hundreds of them, some in suits, some in sweats, some dressed like Ralph Lauren, some dressed like John Gotti, have their faces pressed to the Plexiglas. As if they are at an aquarium. As if they are watching sharks and it's feeding time and the water is full of herring.

These are Pee Wee hockey tryouts in Ridgefield, Connecticut. In the world of youth hockey, Pee Wees are like Britney Spears in that song—not a girl, not yet a woman. Eleven- and twelve-year-olds, tweens, though certain parents, looking for an edge, have been known to stretch it, fake a birth certificate, which, in addition to a diet of greasy food and prescribed pharmaceuticals, explains the occasional behemoth who crosses the ice like a beluga, all shoulders and legs, a sumo among flyweights, which always elicits the same comments from the same parents. "Maybe that kid can lend me his razor." Or "Maybe he'll buy me a beer."

Youth hockey is broken into age divisions, each given a cute name. There must be a history behind these names, though I've never cared enough to find out. Seven- and eight-year-olds are called Mites. Nine- and ten-year-olds are called Squirts. Eleven- and twelve-year-olds are called Pee Wees. Thirteen- and fourteen-year-olds are called Bantams—that's when the game changes. Through Pee Wee, checking is not allowed. Once a kid becomes a Bantam, it's open season.

My son Micah is a first-year Pee Wee, but could pass for a Squirt. He's often lined up against second-year Pee Wees who could pass for Bantam. The height and weight difference can be comical. It dramatizes the story of my people. We are moderately sized. It's always been us against the big fellas. But hockey teaches you a key lesson early: size is not everything. You can beat size with speed or intelligence. Even in the brutal world of youth sports, a smart kid has an edge.

About two hundred prospects turned up at the Ridgefield Winter Garden Ice Arena for the first day of tryouts. It was mid-April. The buds were on the trees, baseball was on the fields, but it was still January in the rink. Kids had come from a half dozen nearby towns. Wilton. Danbury. South Salem. Fairfield. Katonah. Brewster. Some were from farther afield.

These were hotshots, superstars who went from program to program, using each tryout as a practice or an ego boost, a way to humiliate the locals. These kids were from Triple A teams. Parents spoke of their arrival as medieval villagers spoke of nomadic hordes. They are coming! They are coming! From Westchester! From Stamford! From Greenwich! They are coming to pillage and make our kids look silly!

The Fairfield County Amateur Hockey Conference (FCAH) fields four travel teams. From highest to lowest, it goes AA, A, A1, B. The season is long, fifty games culminating in a state tournament. For the parents, this means waking up early, staying up late, and driving for hours. It means living like a long-haul trucker, making the same sort of calculations and drinking the same amounts of coffee. It means visiting each town in the state, coming to know every mascot and jersey as well as the net income, fashion preferences, and pedagogical style of every sort of hockey parent.

Tryouts consist of three sessions over three days. Of the nearly two hundred kids who turned out for day one, seventy will be offered a spot. They will be given twenty-four hours to accept or decline. If they don't respond, the organization will keep their deposit—half the full-season cost, around $1,500. Parents withdraw if they believe their kid has been placed on the wrong team. They might go to another program, where they believe their child will be properly appreciated.

If you have been in the program for more than a year or two, you will know many of the kids at the tryout. You will have studied them in a way an adult should never study another person's child—coldly and cynically, noting each strength and flaw. There's a lot at stake. If your kid makes a top team, he will play with top players. The games will be faster, the opposition better. He will improve just to keep up. He will rise. Choosing a player for a top team can become a self-fulfilling prophecy: Did he make it because he was better, or did he get better because he made it? What's more, the team a kid makes will determine his standing in the youth hockey hierarchy: kids on the AA team rarely fraternize with kids on the B team.

It's even worse for parents. In our program, the adults constitute a tremendous socioeconomic cross section. You see it in all those cars in the lot: Hyundais, Toyotas, Fords, BMWs, three Volvos, two Teslas, and one canary-yellow Lamborghini, owned by a cowboy hat–wearing father in the depths of a midlife crisis. (The pickup trucks belong to the coaches.) You see it in the clothes of the mothers and fathers who line the Plexiglas, which range from bespoke suits to yoga pants, from cashmere pullovers to Target hoodies. Though most of the kids are indeed white—this is starting to change—nearly every income level is represented, every profession, sensibility, and temperament. It's like that *Sesame Street* song "The People in Your Neighborhood." We've got a security guard, a financial adviser, an electrician, a demolition man, a veterinarian, a retiree, a nurse, a pulmonologist, an architect, a contractor, a digger of septic tanks, and a Broadway producer. It's not wealth or fame that determines social position in our neighborhood. It's your child's speed, hands, and "hockey IQ."

If a kid who's been on Single A slips to B, he will be ostracized, his parents cast out. If you talk to them, it's the way you talk to a formerly rich man who has lost everything. You wish you could help, but, really, what can you do? I know a father who cried when his kid didn't make the cut, not because it would hurt his kid, but because it would destroy his own social life. "The Double A parents were my best friends," he said through tears. "Who will I sit with now?"

I'd always heard that a certain kind of sports parent uses their child to fulfill their own unfulfilled childhood dreams; that they live through their nine- or ten-year-old daughters and sons; that they'd only made it so far in sports themselves because they'd been missing a key element, had not worked hard enough or the right way, had given up when they should have pressed on, or had "grown late." Armed with adult knowledge, they'd save their progeny from a similar fate. In this way, they'd vicariously live the life they'd wanted but could not have—the life of the standout, the superstar, the kid who just might go all the way.

And yes, there is some of that. But the motivation for most parents is more immediate. When your kid excels, you are treated better. I'm talking about status, how people greet you as you come through the big double doors into the rink. Once, when my son scored an especially pretty goal, a father climbed out of the bleachers just to shake my hand. I've gotten high-fives, even high-tens. There have been full-body hugs. This is not about the past. It's about right now.

The first tryout session lasted an hour. The parents not pressed against the Plexiglas were in the stands, with steaming cups of coffee. Some took notes. Others were on the phone, giving a blow-by-blow to an absent spouse. There were as many mothers as fathers, and the women seemed, if anything, even more stressed out than the men. ("Why isn't he on his edges? I told him to be on those edges!") Now and then, a mom would shout a bit of instruction, but that's the beauty of hockey: the Plexiglas encloses the ice, protecting the kids from the parents. You can yell, but they can't hear you.

Scattered here and there among the parents were strangers in overcoats, iPads on their laps. In response to the inevitable post-tryout parental blowups, several programs have come to employ "outside evaluators." It's a boom business. These experts make an independent evaluation of each prospect, grading kids from one to ten in a series of categories: inside edge, outside edge, crossover, pivot. It's less about hockey than about skating. The evaluators judge blind—no names, nor stories, nor statistics. Just the randomly assigned numbers on the back of the pinafores passed out at the start of each session. We'd been warned not to interact with the outside evaluators. "Don't even say 'hello.'" When I accidentally approached one of these experts, mistaking him for a college friend, panic came into his eyes, and he said, "Get away, oh please, get away."

When I asked why we used outside evaluators—why not just let the coaches pick their teams?—I was told it was about fairness, impartiality. But since the teams really were picked by the coaches and the parents on the board—FCAH is governed by a democratically elected board—it seemed more likely that the evaluators had been brought in to give the organization plausible deniability. It was something to point to when a parent complained: "It wasn't us. It was them." You got the sense, when you probed, that the expert recommendations came into it only at the margins. The coaches basically knew who they wanted before the first tryout. And those cases in which the outside evaluations did play a role were even more problematic. In fact, tryouts, especially when it came to the nitty-gritty of evaluations, had the same flaws as the rest of the meritocracy. The outside evaluators judge only what can be measured. If it can't be measured, it's as if it doesn't exist. The intangibles, which turn out to be the very qualities that distinguish a good skater from a good hockey player, get lost.

Wised-up parents with money hire private coaches to teach their kid how to excel at the handful of skills measured by the outside evaluators. Edges. Turns. Stride. Like public school instructors, they teach to the test. Over time, the aesthetics of the game have been remade by youth hockey try-outs. All those things that can be measured have improved. The game is faster, the skating more precise, than ever before. All those things that can't be measured have atrophied. Character, leadership, how to deal with boredom or defeat. On the last day of a tournament, in the third period of the seventh game—that's when you'll find the best hockey players. A try-out cannot tell you.

Most of the day-one drills were designed for the evaluators. They are meant to isolate those skills that can be measured. This means five rows of kids executing, at the sound of a whistle, basic maneuvers. Crossover, pivot, sprint, stop—forward, backward. These skills are akin to the primary colors used by a painter: by mixing them, you can do everything that needs to be done in the game. The kids carried the puck only at the end, when they were set against each other in one-on-one, two-on-one, and three-on-two drills. They passed, they shot. The goalies were somewhat exempted. Because there are so few kids who play goalie, they often play for free. They were in the nets for tryouts, giving skaters a way to end a drill, a target—"Go through the cones, then shoot"—but it was only the skating that mattered. And yet the kids spent most of their energy faking out the goalie. They were like a guy on trial playing to the crowd, which has no say in his fate. In short, the kids missed the point, proving my long-held belief that kids are dumb.

I waited with the other parents in the lobby after the session. My son was always one of the last kids out of the locker room, which, especially when it's 4:00 p.m. and dark and the snow is falling on a December afternoon, can be maddening. It's because he likes to hang out with other players, linger and talk. It's because he loves hockey, not just the game but the life. He loves it like a mobster loves Vegas. He'd been playing in Ridgefield since he was five. He was a Mite then, in the house league. He tried out for the travel team as a first-year Squirt. He started on the B team and climbed from there. He now was hoping to make Pee Wee A.

I questioned him as we drove home. I wanted to know how he thought he'd done. At such times, my normally talkative son—on most occasions, I can't get him to shut up—turns into Gary Cooper, strong and silent. He frowns when I question him, then looks away.

"I already told you," he says. "*I don't know!*"

Meanwhile, in a room in back of the Winter Garden, coaches, board members, and outside evaluators were making the first big cut, dividing the kids into two groups: a small group and a big group. The small group consisted of 40—these kids would later be divided into Double A and Single A. The big group consisted of everyone else, 160 or so kids who would later be divided into A1 and B, or cashiered. The cut was not final. An overlooked standout could conceivably jump from the big group to the small, but it was hardly ever done.

The results of day one would be posted on the internet that night—no names, just numbers. Many parents had compiled cheat sheets: the name of each kid beside the pinafore number. That way, they would know the fate of not only their child but also friends' and rivals' children. For the cold-hearted, there is as much pleasure in another's failure as in your own success.

I spent the night with my phone in my lap, hitting refresh. I knew I should not care this much. I knew I had lost perspective. I knew none of it mattered. I knew my son, as good as he was at hockey, was not *that* good—that neither the NHL nor college hockey lay in his future. But I could not help myself. I was reacting at a cellular level. In those hours, I cared about the numbers on that page more than anything else in the world.

The posting was made at 9:00 p.m. I searched the small group for Micah's number. I did not find it. I searched again and again—at first in disbelief, then in confusion, then in fury. I finally spotted it amid the common clay of the big group. I called a half dozen other Pee Wee parents trying to determine who'd made the cut and who, like my son—*look at what they've done to my beautiful boy*—had been shot full of holes. I came to identify with and almost love the parents of those who'd been kept back, and I came to loathe those who'd left us behind.

Only two kids from Micah's Squirt team made the small group, a boy named Brian Rizzo, who played defense, and a kid named Niels Andren, who'd been Micah's rival. Niels played center on the first line for Squirt A. Micah played center on the second line. Micah chased Niels all season but could never catch up. Niels's father, Blake Andren, was a local politician with clout in town, which helped get his kids onto all the top teams. Micah had grappled with Niels in soccer and hockey. Whenever there was a single spot left, it seemed to go to Niels. Meanwhile, Niels's father, Blake, blustery and gregarious, sat with the other top-team parents, not even bothering to watch tryouts. If asked, he'd say, "I'm just the kid's ride." In fact, he seemed certain of the outcome before the tryout began.

The other kid, Brian Rizzo, was the son of the parent-coach Ralph Rizzo, who'd coached Micah for two seasons in Squirts. We were almost friends. Ralph Rizzo looked at Micah and saw a possible obstacle to his dreams for Brian. I looked at Ralph and saw the corruption of America. Ralph made the safest hockey-parent play. He'd signed himself up as a parent-coach, which meant going to classes, getting "certified." Most of the classes were about keeping your mitts off the kinder and watching out for bullies. Many FCAH parents did not play hockey growing up—that lack of firsthand experience could make them insecure and aggressive. Once certified, that changed. The unknowing parent became the all-knowing coach. Ralph was issued a black uniform—pants and jacket, team logo on one arm, his name on the other. Plus a baseball hat. Parent-coaches were merely meant to help the professional head coach—these tended to be men in their twenties or thirties, young fathers who'd played high school hockey—opening the doors to the bench, tending to the injured, directing player traffic. But you put a middle-aged man into that black-and-gold jacket with that all-powerful title on his sleeve—"Coach"—and he is going to exert himself. All to say, Coach Rizzo, who spent the rest of the week selling BMWs at a nearby dealership, entered the Winter Garden like Vince Lombardi entering Lambeau Field. The parents stepped aside, nodded and whispered, "Morning, Coach."

The best youth hockey programs don't let parents coach. It leads to nothing but trouble. The parent-coach either favors his kid or terrorizes him. The standard is higher or lower, but never the same. I have yet to meet the father who can objectively judge his own child; that person doesn't exist. And even if there were such a person, he'd go unrecognized. Why? Because even if there is no conflict, there is still the appearance of conflict, which is almost as bad. In my day—from here on, let it be known that "my day" means the late 1970s and early 1980s—parent-coaches tended to overcompensate. They set a higher bar for their children, made them work harder and more. If you spotted a Little League baseball team with its best player in right field and batting last, you knew it was the coach's kid. Today's parent-coaches tend to do the opposite, using their position to put their kid in the best spot and get him the most at-bats or ice time, for it seems no one will let a single advantage go. This shift—to parents who favor their own from parents who disfavored the same—is part of a general decline in community. As America fades as a dream, it becomes every man for himself.

Team?

What team?

Get your kid to the next level.

That's all that matters.

It was even worse with Coach Rizzo. Not only did he use his position to advance his kid; he used it to hobble others. Having spotted such a kid, he'd short-shift him, scold him when he complained, then tag him with the worst of all labels, "bad kid." As in, "Yeah, I know he can play, but he's a bad kid." I had a sinking sensation as I examined the groupings after that first day: the entire process seemed like theater.

It struck me as I lay in bed that night, angry and unable to sleep: this is America in microcosm. Today's hockey tryouts will be tomorrow's college applications. Today's A team will be tomorrow's Ivy League school. The same people who've wormed their way into this fix will worm their way into that fix, too. Then there was another, even scarier thought: maybe Micah is simply not as good as I think; maybe I've lost all sense of reality; maybe it's not them, but me. I remembered an encounter I'd had with Coach Rizzo a few years back. I'd been complaining about Micah's ice time in Squirts and considered moving him to a different program. "Don't make the classic hockey-parent mistake," he said, "of thinking your kid is always the best." But I told myself that this was not about hockey. Not really. It was about right and wrong. I did not want my son to be cheated. I did not want him to learn, at his age, that the world is corrupt. That knowledge would come soon enough.

I gave him the news in the morning. "You didn't make the top group." I did not want him to find out from Brian Rizzo or Niels Andren at school. I did not want him to learn via gloat. I broke it in the worldly way of my own father: "In life, we learn more from failure than from success." He was bugged but not devastated, or even all that upset.

Which upset me. Why did I care more than he did?

The second tryout session began after school. The locker rooms were a mix of weak players, kids who could barely skate, and kids who'd been shafted: maybe they'd had a bad tryout, or maybe their game was built on intangibles. Or maybe their parents were too opinionated, or maybe they were "bad kids" being taught a lesson by coaches who did not seem to understand the crucial role "bad kids" have played in the history of the game.

I told Micah to just go out there and do his best. "Forget what you can't control, remember what you can. And hustle. The rest will take care of itself." I said this without believing it, which is the job of parents.

I sat in the bleachers beside parents who felt exactly like I did. Each one had a gripe. They bitched and pontificated. Meanwhile, I was trying to see Micah through the eyes of an outside evaluator. Not making the top group seemed to free him. It was as if a weight had been lifted; he was having fun. He began to distinguish himself, began to play his game, which is less about precision than verve. He plays with tremendous style, which is one of the most underrated qualities in sports. It's not just the what; it's the how. Like the slant of sunlight, or the tone of a particular piece of writing. It's what remains when everything else has boiled away. It's a characteristic lope, the joy in the effort. He did especially well during the two-on-one drills. If you put him with a kid who is equally joyful, the game will become what it must have been a hundred years ago, when it was just friends playing on a frozen pond. He scored on a wrist shot, then scored again with a tip-in.

I played hundreds of hours of hockey, baseball, and softball as a kid. I experienced every kind of big moment, and experienced many more as a die-hard Bears, Cubs, Bulls, and Blackhawks fan. I was at the Superdome when the Bears won the Super Bowl in 1986. I was on Lake Shore Drive the following January, the worst time of year in Chicago, when the same team choked on its own blood. A huge Polish cop, standing amid the depressed multitude, said, "Get your heads up. Tomorrow is another fucking day." I lived through the Cubs collapse in 1984. I sat outside my house that night and cried. I was in Cleveland when the Cubs slayed their infamous curse, beating the Indians in the tenth inning of the seventh game of the World Series. I cried that night, too. But nothing in my life as player or spectator has matched the satisfaction I feel when my kid scores a goal. All the while, as the play is developing, I'm expecting him to lose the handle, mess up, as life is indeed mostly failure, but this time he doesn't. I stand and scream when the puck goes in, thinking, "My God, this is how it should always be." It's this feeling that makes parents crazy: having it and not having it and chasing it like a hophead chasing a fix. It's the essence of all sports.

I congratulated Micah after the second tryout. He'd played hard, done his thing, done it well—you can't do more. A friend once told me that you should never tell your kid you're "proud" of him. That makes it about you. He told me you should instead say, "I'm happy for you," which makes it about him. So that's what I said outside the locker room: "I'm happy for you, Micah."

He nodded, smiled, then asked for "candy-machine change."

I ran into Niels's dad, Blake, on my way out. He was chatting up a member of the board. Niels was in the top group, which had its tryout immediately after ours. (The kids in the upper group stood along the Plexiglas watching the lower group while awaiting their turn. Our kids had to walk through them to get off the ice—a tunnel of shame.) Blake shook my hand, frowned, then looked away, saying, "I hope Micah makes it." He said it like a fat cat rejecting a petitioner but wishing him good luck anyway. It infuriated me. Then I saw Coach Rizzo. He was talking to the head coach of Pee Wee A beside the pro shop skate sharpener, which cast his face in a glow of orange sparks. Our eyes met. Then he turned away, pretending he hadn't seen me.

I would have gone over and made him shake my hand, but another parent pulled me aside. This was Rob Laird, whose son Tiger was in the process, though we did not know it, of being relegated to the B team. Laird had been battling the early stages of multiple sclerosis. "The one compensation," he'd said at the time, "is medical marijuana."

Looking into my eyes, he decided there was no one in more need than me.

"Check out a mirror," he said. "You look like one of those guys steering a sixteen-wheeler up a glacier on *Ice Road Truckers*. I wouldn't be surprised to hear someone shout, 'Micah's dad fainted!'"

He handed me a marijuana edible. It was a strip of paper, like a Listerine strip for the soul.

"How does it work?"

"Put it between your bottom lip and teeth and just leave it," he told me.

"How much should I use?"

"One works for me," he said, "but everyone is different. I'd start with a half. Take the rest later if you still need it."

I waited till I got home, then took half, like he said. I put it behind my lip and waited. Laird called thirty minutes later.

"Has it kicked in?"

"Not yet."

"What do you feel?"

"Nothing."

"Just wait," he said.

And then, almost as soon as we got off the phone, it hit me. It came like a wave, like in the old Kool-Aid commercials, a tsunami of punch that lifted me up, then broke over my head. I took the half strip on Thursday at 5:00 p.m. I was high by 5:30 p.m. and remained high for at least three days. Went to sleep high, woke up high. Spent the day high, went back to sleep high, woke up high again. I smoked pot in high school and college, but this was different. That affected my mind. This affected my soul. I began to worry I'd damaged my brain, changed my personality, become like a guy I knew in college who'd taken a hundred hits of acid. For the most part, I enjoyed it. Songs struck me as profound, food was delicious. But now and then I panicked. I wanted it to end. I wanted to feel normal. I had bouts of paranoia. I asked myself, "What the hell did Laird give me? Was that marijuana or was it angel dust?" I reached an insane conclusion: "Micah is in competition with Tiger for one of just a few spots on a top team. The drop has made me paranoid. Laird knows Micah is a better player than Tiger and also knows my counsel is a big part of that, so he's plotted to remove me from the picture. This isn't a medicinal high! It's a chemical lobotomy!"

Even weeks later, long after I believed myself sober, the stony mood would come back, wash over me like a tide. Listening to the radio in my car, I'd think, "My God, this is the greatest song I've ever heard." Then another part of my brain would say, "You've heard this song all your life and know it sucks. Idiot! You're still high!" Sitting in the parking lot of a McDonald's, enjoying myself too much, the same voice would say, "No way these fries are this good. You're still high."

It was through this lens that I viewed the rest of tryouts. It was like watching my kid through the wrong end of a telescope. Everything looked strange, distant, and very small.

I was definitely high when I called Micah's Squirt coach before the final day of tryouts. He'd seen Micah play and knew he belonged on a top team. How did he explain the placement? What did he suggest? He said that Micah did belong on a top team, but to understand him as a player, you had to see him in a game. "Tryouts are not his best," he said. "The kid's a gamer. The next session is all scrimmage, with coaches on the ice. If he plays like he can, he'll be fine."

"We already know you're not making a top team," I told Micah before he suited up. "That part is over. So forget it and just go out and have fun."

Here's a message for test-takers: no matter how hard you work, nor how well you perform, you still need a little luck. In our case, it came as a result of another parent's tactical error.

Blake Andren, believing his son's place was secure on a top team, asked if Niels, who had a scheduling conflict, could spend the final tryout scrimmaging with the lower group, which went on an hour earlier. The coaches agreed, so Micah spent that last day in a kind of showcase, lined up across from the kid who'd been one spot above him on the depth chart all year. It soon became clear: Niels was the better skater, but Micah, who scored twice in the first ten minutes, was the better hockey player.

I was sitting in the bleachers with parents from Micah's Squirt team, lower-tier folks just like me. Most of us had gone through the three stages of tryout grief: denial, anger, acceptance. We were talking quietly, cursing the arrogance of the top dogs, when a man in a dark suit sat down next to me.

"Are you Mr. Cohen?" he asked softly.

I wondered if I'd left on my headlights or parked in a handicapped spot.

"Yes," I said.

"We'd like Micah to play in the second session," he whispered. "Does he have time?"

"Yes," I said. "Of course."

"Good," he said, standing to leave. "And please be discreet."

I suddenly felt estranged from the people around me, lower-tier parents, losers like I used to be.

Christina Egan, with whom I'd been gossiping, leaned over and said, "Did they ask Micah to stay?"

"Yes."

Her lips pursed. She looked at the ice, then said, "Good, that's good."

I called Micah aside as he came off. I told him what happened.

I said, "What was Fonzie?"

He said, "Cool."

I said, "Right. And that's how I want you to be about this."

The hockey played in the second session was crisper and faster. There were twenty-eight kids, not including goalies. They were divided into two teams, then they scrimmaged. Each shift was one minute, the blink of an eye when you're trying to distinguish yourself. It was easy to identify the standouts—several of them would become Micah's teammates: Tommy McDermott and his stepbrother Joey; "Broadway Jenny" Hendrix and "Broadway Julie" Sherman; Barry Meese, the kid with the very old dad; Becky Goodman; Leo Moriarty; and Coach Rizzo's son Brian.

Of course, there were other kids, a handful clearly marked for Double or Triple A—kids so fast and far ahead they seemed untouchable. When two of them went up the ice together, passing the puck back and forth, closing in on the goalie, your heart went into your mouth and you were happy to be there. A friend once told me why basketball fans groan when a half-court shot taken by the other team rims out. "Because you appreciate greatness, even when it hurts."

Micah was stronger in the second session than he'd been in the first—the better the players, the better you play. It's why holding kids back until they are big makes no sense. You never want to be the best kid, or the worst. Dead middle is where the growth is. We went home after and waited. The system seems like it's been designed to create anxiety. *Two hundred kids. Seventy spots.* The Double As are notified first.

It's like a fraternity bid, a tap from Skull and Bones. "We'd like to invite your child to join the Double A Ridgefield Bears." Top players get the initial calls. If they decline, another kid is moved up the depth chart. It takes two or three days to fill the entire Double A roster.

Meanwhile, gossip spreads like a prairie fire. You get an update after each offer has been made. You get the news even if you don't want it. Another mom, another Facebook post: fireworks and champagne bottles. You do the math. The longer you wait, the slimmer the odds. No chance now—it's been thirty-two hours! My expectations adjusted. I was like Rocky, hoping to merely go the distance with Creed. "Nobody's ever gone the distance with Creed." I had no thought of Micah making Double A. It was a miracle he was even in the running for Single A. I'd been sure he'd make it when we left the rink but became less certain as the hours turned into days. Had Micah been pulled up merely because Niels begged out and they needed an extra body? *How cruel!* The call came in the middle of the following week. Micah had made Pee Wee A.

I tried to gloat, but Micah would not let me. He said, "Dad, cut it out." And I did, but he could not stop me from jumping up and down inside. Micah making the team the way he did seemed like a parable, his hockey career in miniature. He'd been judged unfairly and sent down, but persisted, playing himself into the top group, slipping beneath the wire on the last minute of the last day. It *was* like *Rocky*. There was a training sequence, then a showdown. There was a brutalized but victorious fighter calling for his woman, not his wife but his mother, Jessica. ("Yo, Jessica!") And there was me, the cornerman, grizzled old Mickey, on him because I knew what he was capable of. The music should have come up when I got that call, the credits should have rolled, but that's not how life works. It continues instead, triumph giving way to another struggle, more anxiety, more joy.

Hockey is the best sport for kids and parents. Compare it with the others in the marketplace. Start with America's most popular, tackle football. What's wrong with football? How about everything? For one, there is the plethora of positions. It's all specialization, with some kids seeming to matter more than others. For a tackle or guard, the game is not the one you imagine—the pigskin spiraling gracefully through the autumn sky. It's a shoving contest. What does football teach such a kid about life? Devotees think it's teamwork they learn, cooperation and sacrifice. *Bullshit!* They learn the class system. There are the aristocrats—quarterbacks, running backs, receivers, all those who handle the ball—then everyone else, the working masses tasked with protecting the aristocrats. A kid can spend the entire day on the field without touching the ball, and forget about scoring. Then there's the long-term effect of all those collisions, what a few hundred low-impact blows can do to a developing brain. Barack Obama said that if he had a son, he wouldn't let him play. Ditto Terry Bradshaw and Mike Ditka. And look, here comes another Hall of Famer asking if you can help him find his own house! It explains the recent exodus from the game. Many parents who played high school football have pushed their kids into lacrosse and hockey instead. They grew up in another time, in another nation, where football was king. But things change. I recently flew into O'Hare airport. The suburban towns, once dotted with gridirons, were nothing but soccer fields. Driving to Ridgefield's Winter Garden on a fall afternoon, I passed a park where eight- and nine-year-olds were playing tackle football in full gear. If I were a different sort of person, I'd go out there and scream, "Don't any of you people read the newspaper?"

What about basketball, the ranks of which have also been swelled by the dangers of football? It does skirt many of football's problems—contact is incidental, every position is of equal importance, any player can score. But basketball fails in another way. It values height above almost any other quality. A short person, even normal-size, can excel in basketball, but must be wildly gifted to do so, one in a thousand. Height has never been of paramount importance in hockey; with the increasing importance of skating skill, it matters less than ever. Hockey is a refuge for sports parents of moderate stature, like myself. I am five-foot-ten in boots and expect a full-grown Micah to be about the same. The NBA's top 2019 draft pick (Zion Williamson) is six-foot-six, 285 pounds. In the NHL, it was Jack Hughes—five-foot-eleven, 170 pounds.

And what about baseball?

The nation in which that sport was invented and served as a pastime is gone. It's too slow for modern America, too delicate, sophisticated, and subtle to hold the attention of our kids. YouTube and *Fortnite* and the rest have shredded their attention spans. They can't handle all the dead time scattered across a six-inning game, which unfolds over the course of an afternoon. They start with T-ball at age six or seven, then quit. Why? It's boring. And hard. Football, basketball, hockey—there is a place for hustle in these sports, going all-out, forcing the action. Hitting a baseball—if you can't hit, it's no fun—is not like that. Hustle will not help. It's more like belief in God: the harder you try, the harder it gets. You can play hockey angry, with an edge, with a sense of bringing justice to a lawless town, but the opposite is the case when it comes to hitting a baseball. Baseball is like Buddhism. It requires a calm presence. You must clear your mind and concentrate, tune out everything but the ball, which most modern people cannot do.

I have made a study of the kids playing Little League baseball in Fairfield County, Connecticut. I have asked myself, "Just who is out here?" They break into four groups. First, there are the fat kids. Baseball has become a refuge for overweight children whose parents insist they play a sport. Some can barely run. (It's only a matter of time till we bring the designated hitter to Little League.) Second, there are the kids whose fathers or mothers—though, let's be honest, it's mostly fathers—love the game and insist their children play. These kids are unhappy, and quit. Third, there are the kids whose parents immigrated to this country, the sons and daughters of immigrants from India, New Zealand, or China, who believe that to understand America you must play its national game. In short, their information is out-of-date, their participation based on a misunderstanding. They quit, too. Finally, there are the handful of kids who, for whatever cockeyed reason, actually love baseball.

Lacrosse, soccer, tennis? I know little about those sports, those kids, and those parents, but I do know hockey. I know what it has to offer and what it teaches. First of all, it's a tremendous workout. That's why the locker room reeks, why the equipment bag exudes a stench no amount of machine washing can touch. The kids come off the ice sweat-soaked, spent.

Which is itself exhilarating. Exhaust the body, free the soul. Then there's the importance of teamwork. Hockey is about operating together, passing and making plays. A low-skilled group of kids who play as a team will almost always beat an atomized collection of all-stars. That's an invaluable lesson. Here's what it means: teamwork matters more than talent. Or maybe the ability to sublimate your gifts and desires for the good of the team is the talent. When it's functioning like its supposed to, youth hockey is one of the few communities where America still works, where cooperation is rewarded, where the small things count, where it really does come down to who wants it more.

I learned everything from hockey. I started when I was three, playing tape ball with other little brothers at the Deerfield Bubble, home of the Deerfield Falcons, a rink beside the tollway in northern Illinois. My brother taught me to skate there one afternoon. I started on double blades. This was 1972, 1973. Hockey skates were made of soft leather that gave no support. Novices were identified by their ankles. If they bent, you were showered with ridicule. I had a tough time straightening up. As a last resort, my brother, knowing my fear of being run over, got the rink manager to chase me with the Zamboni, the ice resurfacing machine, which advanced like grim death. Fueled by fear, I got off my ankles and on my blades and flew up the ice. That's when I got the nickname my oldest friends still call me, though with sarcasm now: "Rocket." For me, skating has always been connected to the fear of death.

We lived in Libertyville, a farming town thirty miles north of Chicago. We played hockey because the neighbors played and because there was little else to do in winter. No video games, no movie streaming. Other than *Bozo's Circus*, there was nothing on television. So we went to the Bubble, which was on the campus of Trinity International University. It was as sparse as Manitoba, cornfields and sky. At first we played on an outdoor rink enclosed by a chain-link fence. The sky above it was blacker than any sky I'd ever see again. No moon or stars, no worlds out there. Just hockey. At some point, the parents raised money and bought the bubble to cover the rink. It was a tarp, patched here and there, inflated by a massive blower that kept the rink super cold. It was a home ice advantage for Deerfield. Other teams did not think of beating us so much as getting back to the locker room. Once, another kid and I gathered garbage from beneath the bleachers and tossed it into the blower. Candy wrappers, coffee cups, cigarette butts—they made a beautiful arc that rained onto the ice. When players from both teams hit the debris, they lost their edges and went flying. The referee blew the whistle, stopping the clock. He made me and my friend go out on the ice in our sneakers and pick up all that trash.

When the wind came, the bubble shook. On a stormy night while my brother played, it ripped off and flew away. Astonishing! For the parents in the stands, it was as if the roof of the world had been torn off. And there was the sky, re-morseless and black. A posse of mothers and fathers chased the bubble down. It had been expensive; they hoped to salvage it. They caught up with it in Indiana, but by then it had ripped to shreds. A new bubble, with a better design, was in place by the spring.

It wasn't the game I loved so much as the culture of the rink, the crowd around the slot hockey, the locker room gossip, the swagger of a coach whose team had given their best effort, how good a chocolate bar tasted after you played. One kid kept his change in his jock—you could hear him jingle by on the ice. I even loved the way the Coke machine went screwy, dispensing the cup *after* it had dispensed the syrup and ice. This told you about technology. Fewer kids played hockey then, which meant longer drives to the closest rinks, but the drives were the heart and soul of the life.

I started in the house league. That's where most kids played, and as a result, the quality was high. Some of the best kids played house because their parents would not pay for travel. I went out for the Deerfield Falcons, the travel team, as a first-year Squirt. The tryout was tough. There were no more than fifty kids on the ice, but it felt like a million. Drills are now designed to isolate a particular skill: inside edge, outside edge. In my day, drills were designed to see how much a kid could take. Making cuts is unpleasant. How much easier if you can encourage the weak players to quit? A few dozen kids gave up after the first tryout; some actually walked out in the middle. There were no outside evaluators. Players were picked by the coaches, the coach of Double A and the coach of Single A, middle-aged Canadians judging players as they themselves had been judged in Regina or Thunder Bay.

The categories were simple: kids who could play and kids who couldn't. You didn't have to wait long to find out. A coach spoke to us as we changed back into street clothes after each tryout, reading the names of those they wanted to return. Fate was revealed by omission. If you did not hear your name, you were done. My name was called after the first day, after the second, after the third. My brother's teammates stood around me before the last tryout, explaining "what Coach wants to see." It was all scrimmage. I missed an empty net. And I knew. The coach announced the final roster afterward. Twenty-six kids had gotten this far; twenty-four made a team. Another kid and I had to sit like idiots as every other name was read. Kids screamed when they made it. I was crying by the end. I sat in the lobby of the Bubble for an hour, refusing to go home. My mother tried to console me, but I was inconsolable. My brother and his teammates tried to console me—nope. It was my first big disappointment, the first time I'd been told I was not good enough.

My father, who'd been reading the newspaper in the car, came and sat next to me. "I want you to listen to me very clearly," he said. "Life is mostly failure. It's falling short, getting cut, not making teams. It will happen again. It happens to everyone. All you can control is how you react. Everyone gets knocked down. Some people stay down. Others get up. Which will you be?" He put his arm around me, and as he did, the tip of his cigar, glowing like a coal, came dangerously close.

I worked hard all winter, practicing twice a week with a coach named Ray Carmelo. I am still grateful for the things he taught me. I was different when I tried out again. I survived cut after cut and was one of the kids screaming at the end. A week later, I got my first travel jerseys—white with a red falcon for home games, red with a black falcon for away. I got a jacket, too, a red windbreaker with my number, 13, on the sleeve. The jacket made me feel like an aristocrat.

Me on the lower left, looking unaccountably sad.
The Deerfield Bubble, Deerfield, Illinois, Spring 1977

We were coached by a man named Jim Freeberg. When people say you'll be lucky if you have one great teacher in your life, they mean Coach Freeberg. This was the mid-1970s, which explains his big rust-colored beard. If you lost a piece of equipment, you'd look for it in "Coach's beard." He wore bell-bottom jeans, cable-knit sweaters, and his own team jacket. His eyes were shiny and full of mischief. He looked like a hippie but was in fact an evangelist, soberly dedicated to a mission—spreading the game. He'd grown up in Canada but spent his adulthood bringing the good news to hockey-deficient American towns. He was a figure of distinction. In addition to the Squirts, he coached a local high school team, which he'd led to several state championships. He could have coached college kids, even pros, but wanted to work with players at what he considered the crucial moments in their hockey careers—ten years old, seventeen years old, grade school and high school, when they'd either make the game a part of their lives or drift away. He did not expect his kids to play beyond high school, but did want them to remain devotees of the game, which he believed would make them better people.

His methods were old-school. He taught us the game, introduced us to its language and culture. He explained each position and how we were supposed to play it. The center takes the face-off and patrols the middle of the ice and is as responsible for defense as offense. He is supported by his wings—a right wing and a left wing. He called a line with a strong center but weak wings a helicopter, because it flew "without wings." Behind the center are the defensemen—right D and left D. Then the goalie, also known as the backstop or netminder. He or she—the best goalie in Ridgefield is a girl—is said to play "between the pipes."

Coach Freeberg played me at left wing, but I kept drifting right. Realizing I could not discern left from right, he taped a white X on my left glove. "When you don't know where you're going," he said, "follow the X." When I insisted on skating with one hand on my stick, he taped my other glove to the shaft. I was cured. It's from Coach Freeberg that I learned the origin of the term "hat trick"—that's what they call it when a player scores three goals in a single game. It possibly comes from Maple Leaf Gardens, in Toronto, where, in the 1920s, a local haberdasher promised to give a new fedora to anyone who scored three goals that night. It was Coach Freeberg who told us that a natural hat trick means getting those three goals in a row, with no one else scoring between. He told us that a "Gordie Howe hat trick," named for the Detroit Red Wings star, means getting a goal and an assist and having a fight in a single game. Coach Freeberg called the penalty box "the sin bin," called a slap shot a "boomer," called a mustache "lip lettuce," said anyone who was fast had "wheels," and called the sort of goal you scored from a scrum a "garbage goal," adding, "of course there really is no such thing as a garbage goal." He'd knock you down when you got cocky and lift you up when you felt low, saying, "There's still a lot more hockey to play."

For him, a game was a story, a fable with a moral to those who could read it. After we collapsed in the third period one day, he said, "There's nothing more dangerous than a two-goal lead. You think the game is over, when in fact it's never over till it's actually over." After one of our players, having absorbed a cheap shot, delivered a cheap shot in return, he said, "In this game, winning is the only revenge that counts."

A hockey game, for those who don't know, is divided into three periods. A period lasts twelve minutes in Squirt, fifteen minutes in Pee Wee, and twenty minutes in college and pro. The hockey we played in the Bubble was old-time hockey—the game before it was remade by Russian talent. Skate the puck across the red line, dump it into the corner, chase it, and throw it in front of the net, where your teammates bang it in. There was no more ominous phrase than "Man on," which meant that an opponent was shadowing you as you chased the puck. Your opponent's aim? To check you before you could make a pass, to drill you into the boards.

The Squirt A Deerfield Falcons were clicking before the first snow. By mid-December, we were a famed powerhouse, feared throughout Chicagoland. We'd become that most deadly of organizations: a team. No one wanted to disappoint Coach. Everyone wanted to hear him say, "Way to go, gamer."

We sublimated our individual hunger for goals in the service of the greater project. That's when we really started to pass. We blew away the Peoria River Rats, the Quad City Ice Eagles, the St. Jude Knights, and the Buffalo Grove Miners. The Zion Huskies were the only team with a greater home-ice advantage. Their rink was on the fence line of the Zion nuclear station, their parking lot in the shadow of the cooling tower. Every time the horn blew, we flinched, fearing a meltdown. We were less concerned with winning than with escaping with our reproductive systems intact. "Don't get irradiated" was the order of the day. Some Deerfield parents came up with a cheer:

> *We don't care*
> *If we score*
> *As long as water*
> *stays in the core!*

Yet we did win, and kept on winning. We made it all the way to the Illinois State Championship, which was played at the home of the Chicago Cougars, a semipro team. Nine thousand seats, a four-sided scoreboard above center ice. We were introduced like pros, our names announced over the loudspeaker as our faces flashed on the monitor. "And now, playing left wing for the Falcons, Richard 'Rocket' Cohen!"

The game was a barn burner. The lead changed hands again and again. It was tied late in the third period when I got out on the ice. I was skating up the left side, hoping not to make a mistake, not to screw up. The thought of letting down Coach terrified me. Our right D dumped the puck into the corner. Our right wing threw it toward the net. Our center took a shot, which their goalie deflected. I picked up the rebound, went behind the net, and jammed it in from the right side. They call this a wraparound; it ended the game. My teammates swarmed me. "Here's the game winner," Coach Freeberg said, handing me the puck in the locker room. My goal was shown on TV that night after a Cubs spring-training report. It was at the end of the news, comic relief, but that's not how it felt. It felt like the biggest thing that had ever happened.

It was my last season as a Falcon. My family had moved up the lake to Glencoe, and my mother refused to make the drive to Deerfield three nights a week. If I wanted to play, she said, it'd have to be for the local team, the Winnetka Warriors. This was like a football player switching, mid-career, from the Patriots to the Bengals. It meant going from the top to the bottom. It wasn't just the Winnetka Pee Wees—I was now a Pee Wee—but the entire organization that stank. Deerfield was a hockey powerhouse. Winnetka was a loser at every age level. The Winnetka kids knew about me before the tryout, because I'd played at Deerfield. They called me "Mr. Deerfield." When I got to practice, one kid—his name was Ethan and he had a wispy blond mustache—always asked if I'd come "from the synagogue." There was a mistake with our jerseys. On half of them, the Warrior's logo—the flying *W*—had been printed upside down. People called us the M's. We were coached by a parent, a big, angry stock trader named Jim Campbell. He had intense eyes and shattered blood vessels all over his face. He wore the sort of glasses you might find in the Jeffrey Dahmer collection. You never knew what you were going to get. On some nights, he was warm and encouraging. On others, he was punitive and mean. I later learned that he'd been going through a divorce and was self-medicating. He drove a Harley. Once, when his bike fell over, he made us go out and stand it up.

"Consider this part of your training," he said.

He made me alternate captain. After I'd blown a scoring chance, he cut the *A* off my jersey with a Swiss Army knife, saying, "You don't deserve it, Mr. Deerfield."

We lost fifteen games in row. Then won. The other team was demoralized, knowing they'd lost to a team that had lost fifteen games in a row. We stood beside them after the horn, waiting for someone to find the key to the dressing rooms. Kids on our team started singing "We Are the Champions." When they got to the part that goes "no time for losers," they pointed at the other team, and a melee ensued.

That's me, bottom row, second from the left. Winnetka Ice Arena, Winnetka, Illinois, Winter 1980

That season did not make me hate hockey, but it did kill the love. The wrong coach at the wrong time can do that. That's why I was involved with Micah's team in a way my parents had never been with mine. That's what I told myself anyway. I was on the lookout for the wrong coach, who I knew would come.

And yet I played on. In high school. In college. In New York's adult leagues at the Sky Rink at Chelsea Piers. My team was called Blind Justice. Our jersey showed a blindfolded lady holding a hockey stick instead of scales. This team represented the Manhattan District Attorney's Office, though most of the players weren't lawyers. They were janitors, security guards, paralegals. My brother, who worked for the U.S. attorney, wormed his way onto the roster and brought me along. It was exciting to stand in the traffic of Hudson Street with your hockey bag and sticks, waiting for a cab. It was exciting to step out of the rink into a cool Manhattan night.

The quality of play was uneven. There were a handful of good players, guys who'd played in high school or college, but many more who'd learned on Rollerblades or from Nintendo's *Blades of Steel*. Some of them could barely get up and down the ice. Worst were guys who knew the game only from television. They believed that fighting was a regular part of the sport, that the night was not complete till you'd dropped the gloves. Until then, I'd never been in a hockey fight; now here I was, at one in the morning, being whacked by a hedge fund manager who kept saying, "Wanna go?"

The late games had a desperate feel. *This is how your hockey life ends.* One night, one of our defensemen, a prosecutor named Steve Brostoff, was penalized for cross-checking. The call was questionable, which did not justify Brostoff's tirade.

He cursed all the way to the penalty box, where he took his helmet off and went on cursing.

"Hey, ref," he screamed, "you're a disgrace to that uniform."

The ref skated over.

"It's midnight, and I'm reffing you assholes for minimum wage," he told Brostoff. "I'm a disgrace all right, but it has nothing to do with this uniform."

Our captain was named Steve Caro. He was a contractor at the U.S. Attorney's Office. If you needed a shelf, you called Caro. He stood outside the Sky Rink with a clipboard, calling out names as each player arrived. In a thick Brooklyn accent, he'd say, "Hey, Richie? Richie? Hey, Richie? Ya here?" He made the question seem profound: Was I here? If so, why? What was I doing with my life?

At some point, my brother took over the team. He liked pep talks. He'd say, "We can do this, boys. We just have to want it! Do you want it?" He began to use me as a counter-example: "See what my brother did? Do the opposite." He'd scream at me for missing an open net, scream at me for not passing, scream at me for passing too much. I'd be furious when I got home at two in the morning, then lie awake for the rest of the night muttering. I wanted justice. It was only when I understood that there is no such thing as justice, not in this world, that I realized I could quit hockey and go on with my life.

Blind Justice won the championship of the Chelsea Piers Division III men's hockey league in my last season. Credit me. I'd recruited two recent college grads who made the difference. It was not that they were better, but that they were so much younger. They blazed with new engines in new bodies while the rest of us sputtered and broke down. Each year I was slower and clumsier than I'd been the year before. At a certain point, I realized I'd been better at twelve than I was at thirty-five. That's when I decided to quit all activities in which my abilities were on the wane—binge drinking, recreational drug use, ice hockey—and instead focus on those areas where there was still room for improvement: guitar and golf. I got married, had kids—more kids than I'd expected. I had one son. Then I had three. Now I have four. When I say four, some people look at me with respect, others in disgust. (Perhaps I will write a memoir called *The Accidental Hasid*.) I did not want to leave the city but could not afford to stay. I'd procreated my way out of town. As soon as that third kid was born, a white ball sucked me up and carried me to Connecticut. I knew nothing about my new state or town, or any of those nearby. My wife and I'd picked Ridgefield like we'd pulled a name from a hat. I'd seek out people with roots in Chicago and ask, "Where are we? Is this Winnetka or more like Deerfield? Or Schaumburg? Highwood? Wait a second—are we in Libertyville? It's Libertyville, isn't it? Or is it Glen Ellyn? My God, am I living in Glen Ellyn?"

I got to know Ridgefield by living in Ridgefield. It's a beautiful, storybook New England town with a tree-lined Main Street, ponds, and what my father calls "rolling hills." Everything from my old life seemed to follow me here. Bands I'd listened to in high school (Squeeze, Erasure) turned up on a senior circuit that went through a theater a mile from our new house. I spotted a hockey rink about a thousand yards from my front door. The Winter Garden—it's out of my past, Deerfield Bubble vintage, with a rickety roof and a single sheet of ice. It was like Brigadoon for me, a vision that appears only when you absolutely need it. As soon as I saw the rink, I knew my hockey life was not over. I had quit the game, but it had not quit me. I also knew I'd changed roles. I'd been a player. Now I'd be that most terrifying of monsters, a hockey parent.

I started with my oldest son, Aaron, who was six at the time. I did not ask permission, nor talk it over with my wife. I simply signed him up. I was now my father, my son was now me. In this town, you start with Ice Mice, which consists of a few dozen tiny kids in oversize gear pushing toys around the ice. We were lucky to find a great teacher, Cathy Bonner, who got our kids to love skating, even if they did not always love hockey. Aaron was a natural on blades. He played a season in the house league, then I signed him up for travel. Tryouts lasted two days. He made the Ridgefield Mite B Team, then climbed to A1.

I'd volunteered to coach. After all, this was said to be the whole point: father and child together on the ice and on the road. But I was a bad coach, moody and aloof. I'd never been a leader. I'm a slave to the chemicals in my brain, that great tidal flow. Sometimes happy, sometimes angry, sometimes sad. I attribute this to a strain of mental illness that runs in my family, along with birth order. My sister is the oldest. She's a lawyer. She stands before juries making her case. My brother is the middle, betwixt and between. I am the youngest, the slacker who stands back, observes, and reports. For a freelance writer, life is a sick day without end. I imagined being a different sort of person as a coach. I'd skate beside Aaron and his teammates, guiding them through the particulars of the game, but I was in fact impatient. I could never clearly explain what I wanted them to do, or get them to do it. It was even worse with Aaron. I never forgot that I loved him, but I could only see what he was doing wrong.

And the other parents drove me nuts. Most had never played, yet they were all experts. They wanted me to teach their eight-year-olds how to take a slap shot, though such shots were verboten till Pee Wee. I told them it was unnecessary as well as forbidden—a player can live an entire hockey life, even play in the NHL, without ever developing a slap shot. But to them hockey meant slap shots, and I was raining on their parade. In this way, they came to distrust me, then dislike me. I didn't blame them. I didn't like myself very much that season.

The games could be unbearable, especially considering how long it took to get to some of the rinks. It was less hockey and more like a drunken dream of hockey. Aaron handled the puck well but, for whatever reason, didn't seem to get the point of the game. He was involved in a kind of parallel play. If the action was here, he was over there; if the action went over there, he came back here. He shied away from contact and never felt the urgency. Now and then, though there were no goalies in Mites, he'd station himself in the net, as if guarding a bank that had not yet been built. It seemed like abdication.

When I asked about it later, he said, "I was protecting."

"What were you protecting," I demanded. "What?"

All those skills—crossovers, backward pivots—are merely

tools meant to help you score. He never seemed to accept that. He skated in a bubble, happily lost in his own world.

Near the end of Aaron's hockey career, we played in a tournament in West Hartford. A Sunday in November, the worst time of year. The leaves had fallen, the highways were black. The parents sat in the locker room with their kids before the last game, bullshitting. They chatted as they filed out, men swaggering in flannel. Then they filed back in, only now quiet and pale. Something terrible had happened.

"What's going on?" I asked.

"Do you know who's coaching the other team?"

"No. Who?"

"Messier."

Mark Messier played in the NHL from 1979 to 2004. He was one the best forwards in history, a Gordie Howe–like All-Star who, like Gordie Howe, could score, assist, and brawl. He'd been a champion and a captain in Edmonton and New York. In 1994, when the Rangers faced elimination in game six of the Stanley Cup semifinals, Messier guaranteed victory, then backed it up by scoring three times in the third period against the New Jersey Devils. It was not just how Messier played that intimidated people, but the way he looked. He has high cheekbones and dark, almond-shaped eyes and chiseled features. Even in repose he seems to be glowering. He can't help it. It's his face. He did not mess around with the puck when he played—no dipsy-doodle for the captain. When he got the puck, he went to the net by the shortest route possible. He never lost sight of the game's essential object: to score more goals. He collected forty-three points in his last season, when he was forty-three years old. He'd slimmed down since retirement—was bald, tall, and handsome, but still 100 percent

Messier. He'd helped establish a youth hockey program in Greenwich, Connecticut, where his son played. He was presumably coaching for the same reason as me: togetherness.

We scored three goals in the first period, building a lead that seemed insurmountable. I looked over at Messier. He looked back—he was wearing jeans and a long, black coat—and nodded.

By God, he nodded!

I called my wife between periods. You're not supposed to use a phone on the bench, but I couldn't help it. "I just wanted you to know that we're playing Mark Messier's team and we're going to win," I told her. "I am going to beat Messier!"

We would've won, too, if not for the most ostentatious celebration I've ever seen. A kid whose name I forget scored early in the second period, putting us ahead 4–0. He pumped his fist when the puck went in—which, fine—then did a routine that covered the entire ice. He pointed at every kid on the Greenwich bench, rode his stick like a pony, did the robot, and gave his goal to God, at which point, Messier, who had not seemed all that engaged in the game, called a time-out. He said a few words to his players, then made some adjustments. A Greenwich kid who'd been sitting out tightened his skates and went onto the ice. Messier's son Douglas moved from defense to center. He won the face-off, then scored. He scored again, then again. When it was over, Greenwich had beaten us by six goals. Our parents waited at the rink door to shake Messier's hand. Parents are normally quiet after a thumping. Ours were giddy. They said things like, "Great game, Mr. Messier. It's not who wins or loses, right, Mr. Messier?" Being at the rink with the Hall of Famer seemed to justify every decision they'd ever made. The schools they'd attended, the jobs they'd accepted, the people they'd married—every choice had been correct because it led them here, to the same place as Mark Messier.

I was not in such high spirits. It was a dark autumn night with a cold front moving in. I carried Aaron's equipment bag to the minivan, then stood over the hatchback trying to make it fit. I felt something roll up beside me, the humming presence of an elegant machine. I looked over. It was the Messiers—Mark and Douglas—in a low-riding car, possibly a Maserati. Messier flashed me a peace sign, or maybe it was *V* for "victory," then roared off. Watching his taillights, I said to myself, "Fuck you, Messier."

Aaron and I drove in silence. The game encapsulated our entire situation. Hockey was my passion, not his. He did not like it, but pretended to for me. I knew he didn't like it, but pretended to believe he liked it, for him. We were living a lie, but I couldn't find a graceful way out. Finally, because he is more adult than I am, Aaron came to me and said, "Dad, I don't want to play anymore. I'm done."

I tried again with my second-born, Nate, but not with as much determination. My ass had been whipped by reality. I was in no hurry to have it whipped again. But I did want him to give it a try. I signed him up for Ice Mice. I won't go into detail, but suffice to say Nate did not take to the game. Getting him into the gear was like getting a dog into a sweater. His arms went straight, his legs turned stiff, and he stared at me with hatred. I came back from the rink wiser. I'd finally realized that you can't make a person do what they don't want to do, especially if it's your own kid. You can't tell them what to care about, be interested in, or love. They come into the world hardwired. The most you can do is clear the path. There is no invention, just discovery.

I'd given up on hockey by the time Micah was in school. He found the game on his own, which is probably why he loved it. He started to play by following his friends to the rink. My wife signed him up for house league. I refused to buy new equipment. I told him to search among the discarded junk in the garage instead, that depository of faded dreams. I did not go to his games. My wife dropped him off or he got a ride with friends. I'd stopped caring about hockey.

It's hard to really see your own kid play anyway. It's like trying to see the Grand Canyon free of expectations. In the end, it's not the Grand Canyon you see but yourself seeing the Grand Canyon. It's like that watching your kid play hockey. You see only the positives or negatives. As a result, you will, depending on your personality, think your kid is the best or the worst. Almost no parent thinks their kid is in the middle, not great, not awful, just average, which most of them surely are. If you want the truth, it's best to wander into the rink by accident and see your kid without knowing what you are seeing.

My wife asked me to pick Micah up at the Winter Garden one day. He was supposed to be outside. I parked and waited, then got annoyed and went in. My eyes went straight to the ice, where a kid was carrying the puck. He faked his way around two forwards and was one-on-one with a defenseman when another kid knocked him down. It was only then, as I was still admiring the play, that I realized I'd been watching my own kid.

AUGUST

The storms blow in from the south. It's strange to feel a Caribbean wind in Connecticut, that hurricane ache as the clouds pile up and the sky darkens. The owners of the Winter Garden melt the ice in May and keep the rink closed for half the summer. The Zamboni is locked up, the cones and nets put away. The rink is shadowy, its doors wound in padlocked chain. The town itself is given to indolence, awnings shade Main Street, the schools are empty. Certain words linger: "sleepy," "inert." Sitting beside a pond, you can almost believe that life here has not changed in two hundred years. It's the same kids and the same dreams, the same men fishing for descendants of the same fish in the same waterways, the same shade on the same roads, the same banjo frogs in the same vernal pools.

What happens to hockey kids and their families in the summer?

If casual and sane, they turn back into ordinary Americans, put on bathing suits and flip-flops and head to the beach, play Wiffle ball, swim and sail, walk in a pack through town, go to the shorefront cottages of grandparents or camping in the White Mountains with overly enthusiastic uncles.

We used to hang up our skates in April and not think about them again until the first cold night of autumn. By August, hockey was a memory from another life. But America has changed. Downtime has been banished. Kids used to play everything; now they're encouraged to focus like a laser on a single sport. Blame Malcolm Gladwell, who, in his book *Outliers: The Story of Success*, says that a person must practice for ten thousand hours to master anything, the assumption being that if you do practice for ten thousand hours, you will become a master. Gladwell lays out a program in those pages, a way to turn a kid into a star. Millions of tiny athletes have been held back as a result. The parents tell you it's because their baseball- or football-loving son or daughter had not been "mature" enough for kindergarten at the time, had not been "ready," but there's a more prosaic reason: by waiting a year, the parent had, as per Gladwell, made their kid the oldest in class, thus the biggest and most developed in their game, giving her or him a better shot at making the top teams, meaning more and better coaching, the result being a confidence that just might carry him or her all the way! Of course, she or he will still need to put in the work, which is yet another reason to focus on a single sport. It's the fastest way to accumulate the all-important ten thousand hours.

Gladwell is a guru, heeded by people who have grown tired of waiting. In the process, parents have remade the game in the image of the adult world, turned it into work. When hockey season ends, many kids continue with spring leagues and summer clinics, followed by sleepaway hockey camps. There is no off-season, just as there is no summer inside a rink. When you see those kids in the fall, they look as pasty as workaholics. They have grown as players, and all it cost was a summer of their childhood.

We had our first team meeting in mid-August, just the parents, twenty or so middle-aged adults dragging themselves across the sunstruck parking lot of the Winter Garden. Too hot, too soon. The season always catches you by surprise, before you are ready. We sat in a windowless room filled with detritus—broken nets, smashed wipe boards, and other relics of the life. We'd expected to meet the coach but were greeted by a bureaucrat instead. Certain incidents from the previous season, most having to do with the Bantams—a kid was cursed out by another kid's mom; a Darien player was, at the instruction of a Ridgefield father, knocked down with a vicious blindside check; a Bears' coach was supposedly offered a bribe and, had it not been so chintzy, might have taken it—required instruction and correction.

FCAH's parent board had hired a service called Hockey Fix, which, when an alarm is sounded, dispatches counselors to meet with parents and remind them what really matters. Here's another sign of societal breakdown: what's no longer taught at home must be imported via a fee-charging service, which sent two men, a guy in khakis and his assistant, who handed out worksheets and pencils.

The top guy gave a potted speech. He started with youth sports in general, their history and purpose in American life, then went into hockey in particular, then went into the incidents that had tainted our program. He talked about the rules that FCAH parents would now be required to follow. Some were common sense and universal: Don't curse in the stands. Don't heckle or challenge referees. Respect all coaches and kids. Others had been invented for us: no cash gifts; no comments regarding gender, religion, or ethnicity; no secret meetings. He said the chances of any of our kids playing college hockey were negligible, "so forget about that right now—this game is not paying your child's way through university. The kids who will play college are probably not in this program. For your kids, *these* are the golden days. Don't ruin it with your fantasies."

"Turn to the back page of your workbooks," he continued, "where you will find a list of goals."

He wrote the goals in block letters on a wipe board:

> Winning
> Fitness
> Learning to play hockey
> Learning to appreciate hockey
> Teamwork
> Fun
> Self-confidence
> Memories

He told us to assign a number to each goal, ordering them in importance. He gave us five minutes to do this, then asked several parents to read their rankings out loud. Though he said, "There are no wrong answers," he proceeded to tell us why our answers were in fact wrong. "Fun comes first," he said. "Winning is last. There's wiggle room with some of the others, but in general, teamwork should come before fitness, self-confidence should come before learning to appreciate hockey."

There was a heated exchange when Alan Hendrix, one of our team's parent-coaches, argued that "fun" could not be first if "winning" was last.

"I don't know if you've ever been in a locker room," Coach Hendrix said, "but if you're only losing, it's not going to be very fun."

"It's not either/or," the counselor said. "We don't *dismiss* winning. We just don't make it a priority. If you put winning before these other things, your kids will not have a good experience. And they will probably lose anyway. If you emphasize teamwork and fun, they will win. It's an effect, not a cause. Does that make sense?"

Most of the parents were more interested in the other parents—what they looked like and did, who they were. That was the meeting's real takeaway. Text: Don't lose your sense of proportion; remember this is all about the kids. Subtext: So this is who I'll be stuck with for the next seven months.

If your kid plays a travel sport, you'll end up spending more time with the other parents than you have with any group of strangers since high school—hours at the rink and on the road, meetings, practices, and tournaments. You become a kind of pop-up society. You can spot these groups at a distance. They gather in a circle in the lobby of the rink before games; they talk in low voices, facing in. This arrangement is to youth hockey what the confessional is to church or the huddle is to football. It's a sacred space, where we share our irritations, hopes, and fears. I call it the holy hockey circle.

The majority of Pee Wee A parents were white. Otherwise, they seemed, as I've said, to represent a fairly broad American cross section:

There was Judd Meese, rich and retired with a young wife and a young son named Barry. Judd, who would be eighty before Barry finished college, came from a renowned old New England family. Judd's grandfather had been an industrialist and an ambassador. Judd's father founded one of America's most prestigious literary magazines. Judd spent most of his time pursuing his passion—aviation. He bought, restored, and flew vintage aircraft. He showed me pictures of the World War I–era Curtiss JN-4 biplane he flew over the Hudson River Valley.

Barry Meese seemed to drive his own hockey career, dragging his father along. They spent part of every summer day at the Sono Ice House in Norwalk, Judd reading back issues of *Plane & Pilot* as Barry worked with a private instructor. A quiet, craggy presence in the bleachers, Judd did not talk during games. He kept score in a notebook instead, recording every goal, assist, and penalty. He was our unofficial data guy. I later learned he'd only recently begun keeping score. It was a strategy, a way to control his emotions. "He used to be a screamer," one parent told me. "He got kicked out of the rink in Bridgeport. It was a reality check. He started keeping score after that."

Parent-coach Alan Hendrix was a security officer at PepsiCo in Purchase, New York. His wife, Grace, an executive at Pepsi, was freckle-faced and small, with black eyes and Coke-bottle glasses. Their daughter Jenny—the kids called her "Broadway Jenny" because she was obsessed with show tunes and could name and sing every song that appeared in certain Broadway productions—was one of three girls on the team. In recent years, especially as the game has come to reward speed and smarts over size and force, girls have become an ever bigger presence in what had been boy's youth hockey. There are all-girl teams, but many parents prefer that their daughters play with the toughest competition, which tends to mean playing with boys. Why? Because the better the players, the better the play. This has been good for the boys as well as the girls—it's rid them of many of the gender assumptions that warped the minds of previous generations, like mine. In uniform and equipment, you can't even tell the boys from the girls. Often, it's only the hair that gives them away.

Jenny Hendrix was small, like her mom. The grown-ups called her the Energizer Bunny. Tough and determined, she never stopped moving. Cross-checked or tripped to the ice, she'd pop up like a Weeble. Some kids are motivated by a love for the game. Jenny was motivated at least partly by fear of her father, who called out even her smallest mistake, blaming her for things that weren't really her fault.

There were Jocko and Camille Arcus, gearhead car enthusiasts who'd met at Lime Rock, the racetrack in Lakeville, Connecticut. They crisscrossed the travel hockey world in a 1968 vermillion green Dodge Charger as Dan, their child and our Hoover Vacuum of a goalie, dozed in the back seat. Jocko was burly, bearded, bejeweled, tattooed, and very happy. He walked with a limp, which he'd apologize for, saying, "Someday, I'll tell you my story." Camille was pretty, and tired of it all. They lived in a distant blue-collar town and traveled hundreds of miles each week for practices and games.

Parky Taylor was a private equity guy—like just about every other private equity guy, he talked constantly about how much he hated his job. He'd grown up in Darien, Connecticut, which, he often told us, "is fancier than Ridgefield." He'd lived in London and New York City before returning to Fairfield County to raise his family. A lot of our games were played at prep schools, about half of which Parky had attended. He'd look around as we came in the door and say, "I got kicked out of here, too." He was married to Jill, whose grandfather played in the NHL in the 1960s. This meant that Parky's son Duffy, maybe the most skilled Pee Wee in town, had royal blood. He was eligible for the throne. But like an epic hero, Duffy had a fatal flaw. For Odysseus, it was pride. For Duffy, it was temper. The kid could not control his rage.

Bobby McDermott was a beer importer. He knew more about hockey than the rest of us combined, which is why he hardly ever spoke. As Lao Tzu said, "He who knows does not speak; he who speaks does not know." Bobby, who grew up in suburban Toronto, played two seasons of Juniors in the notoriously rough Western Hockey League, which includes teams from Regina, Moose Jaw, Swift Current, and Red Deer, Canada. Bobby had the look of an enforcer—stoic with short red hair and scars. He had two kids on the team—one biological (Tommy) and one via his second marriage (Joey). His wife, Eunice, who told us she couldn't care less about hockey, hardly ever came around.

Simone Camus was a French physicist sent by the government in Paris to explain the most recent developments in particle science to her American counterparts at Yale. From what I understood, she came directly from the Large Hadron Collider near Geneva, Switzerland, where she'd been part of the team that detected the so-called God particle. She'd been in Ridgefield for three years, in which time her son, Jean, had, to her horror, become Americanized. He wore a Mets cap, loved pro wrestling, and insisted on being called Jack. Jack Camus had once been among the best players in the program, but an injury, suffered at the beginning of his second Squirt year, knocked him off his game. He'd been badly concussed by a cheap shot. He'd recovered physically, but the injury made him timid. He steered clear of corners, avoided physical contact, and at times even seemed scared of the puck. A survival instinct is great for longevity but terrible for your hockey. Jack fell from the first line to the third after the injury, shedding status along the way. Simone had become an outcast as a result, though she did not seem to know it. A single mother, probably a genius, she was treated dismissively by parents and coaches, especially Ralph Rizzo, who'd given up on her as soon as he was certain she would never buy a BMW. "I offered her a great deal, but she's just as scared as her kid," he told me.

Albert Moriarty was an FBI agent out of New Haven. His son Leo was only half dedicated to hockey; he was a standout lacrosse player and now and then missed hockey games to attend lacrosse matches. In other words, he was not only cheating on hockey—he actually seemed to prefer the mistress! Though he could skate and shoot, Leo was the most suspect sort, a player of two games, a sports bigamist in an age of specialization. "If that boy isn't committed to us," Coach Hendrix asked, "why should we be committed to him?"

Sue Campi was a dental hygienist in Danbury. At one point or another, she'd cleaned the teeth of every kid on the team. She split parenting time with her ex-husband, Gordon, whom I did not like at first but later came to love. That's the way it is on the adult side of the youth game: you start out hating these people, because in them you recognize your own worst qualities, but end up loving them for the same reason. Gordon worked as the American distributor for a French cheese consortium. He brought samples of gaperon and Camembert to games, offering to give a wedge to the parents of any kid who "puts in more than four." Gordon and Sue's son Patrick, tall and earnest, was having trouble making the transition from defense to offense. He was a good player but had little instinct for scoring.

And there was Jerry Sherman, who would become my confidant. He was a bear of a man, wore thick glasses, and laughed all the time. His suits looked like they came off the rack at the Big and Tall Men's shop. He'd take his coat off in rinks, but his hat—a winter hat, complete with pom-pom—never left his head. Though he was a fairly well-known theatrical producer—you might remember his show *The Green Awning*—he seemingly spent most of his time sending funny texts. He was the only parent to take advantage of the travel part of travel hockey. During a tournament in Philly, he dragged his daughter Broadway Julie on a tour of a nearby Civil War battlefield. In the course of the season, Jerry and Broadway Julie toured the PEZ Visitor Center, the Mark Twain House, and the Peabody Museum at Yale, "to see that big goddamn dinosaur."

Most of the other parents were involved in finance. If they did not work at trading houses or banks, they managed hedge funds, worked for companies that insured those funds, or worked for regulators that policed them. To these people, Ridgefield was a bedroom community—they spent the working day in glass office buildings in Westport, Stamford, Greenwich. To the kids of these bankers, the adult world was money. There's a connection between banking and hockey.

For the children of finance, hockey is *the* game. Maybe it has to do with the neatness of life on the ice, the importance of the clock, or the invariance of the physical environment— always cold, always winter—or maybe it's economics. To play basketball, you need only a pair of sneakers. It costs thousands just to gear a kid up for hockey and thousands more to put him on a good team. A typical travel season will set you back at least ten grand.

I was the only writer among the parents, the only person in the business of turning out a product for which there was little market and no need. It made me an oddball. When you tell people you're a writer, they assume you're unemployed. When they find out you actually earn a living, they chuck you on the shoulder and say, "Terrific!"

We were asked to sign a pledge at the end of the meeting. In it, we promised to "follow the rules of conduct, to neither heckle nor throw items from the stands, to neither engage in taunting nor fisticuffs, to neither seek preferential treatment for ourselves or our children, but in all ways set a good example." We agreed to wait twenty-four hours before discussing a game or game decisions with any of the coaches. The "twenty-four-hour rule" was said to be of paramount importance. "I think you'll find that, a day or two later, you won't even remember what was bothering you," the Hockey Fix counselor told us.

This turned out to be true almost all the time.

We met our kids' head coach at a local bar a few days later. His name was Pete Wilson, but he told us to call him Coach

Pete. He was closer in age to the players than to the parents, boyish with a lock of hair that swung across his forehead like a pendulum. He was of average height, carried himself like an athlete, and looked like a hockey player, which was comforting. Unlike the parent-coaches, he did not wear much official gear, but favored jeans, sneakers, and sweatshirts. We knew his particulars from the FCAH website, where the bio and headshot of every coach was posted. According to this official history, Coach Pete was twenty-five years old, a newly married accountant. He grew up in Ridgefield, where he played high school hockey. Whereas other programs boasted coaches who'd played in college or even professionally, Ridgefield was run by locals, by townies, who'd been coached by locals in their time.

Of course, having been a great player doesn't mean you'll be a great or even a good coach. The opposite may be closer to true. For a great player, the game comes naturally, instinctually, making it hard to teach. It's impossible to explain what you don't remember learning. The kids who have to work the hardest can frustrate a great player turned coach. He will scratch his head, then say, "Don't do that." Or, "Goddamnit, just score!" You'd rather have a coach who never played but knows how to talk to kids. Coach Pete did not fit in either school. He'd been a middling high school player who loved hockey but did not really like to talk at all. He was self-effacing, distracted. This probably had to do with his unofficial bio, which only a few of us knew. His father and older brother had been beloved Ridgefield coaches. Charismatic and kind, they were something like "made men" in town. If you mentioned "Coach Wilson" around older parents, they'd smile and ask, "Is your boy being coached by Old Buck Wilson?"

"No, his son."

"Bobby? Heck, he's even better than Old Buck!"

"No. The *little* brother."

"There's another Wilson?"

Coach Pete had spent a single season behind the bench when he took over the Pee Wee A team. He'd worked as an assistant for his brother, who coached the Midget Double As. This would be Pete's first season as a head coach, but that was not the part of the unofficial bio that would impact our season. What I have in mind could be followed in the local newspapers, though no parent other than me seemed to.

After decades of coaching hockey and running an investment firm in Westport, Coach Pete's father, Old Buck Wilson, fell in love with a client who was even younger than Coach Pete. In the process of wooing and keeping this woman, Old Buck, who had a wife and several children, betrayed several oaths he'd sworn to uphold. In the end, to pay for jewels and outfits, vacations and houses, Old Buck first emptied his own accounts, then stole from clients, even his kids. He would be convicted of embezzlement, breach of trust, tax evasion, and other financial crimes, and sentenced to prison. This story was splashed across Danbury's *The News-Times*.

Coach Pete had only a few rules, which he explained at that first meeting. Players must arrive an hour before games, a half hour before practices. They must wear a tie and khakis to tournaments. "Complaints about playing time will not be tolerated," he added. "If a parent complains, I will ignore it. If a kid complains, he or she will be benched. And you already know about the twenty-four-hour rule."

The team had its first practice a few days later. Last week of August, ninety degrees in the shade. The ice was damp in the corners. The kids surprised me with their speed, size, and skill. It's amazing what a summer of growth can do. They flew through drills, then broke into lines to work on game situations: three forwards facing two defensemen. Pass, pass, pass—shoot! If all went well, the puck made the goalie's water bottle—always placed on top of the net—jump.

Coach Pete was on the ice with the kids, as were the parent-coaches. Coach Alan Hendrix raced up and down beside the Pee Wees. He had the intensity of a parent who takes out an eight-year-old in a father-son game. Coach Ralph Rizzo stood back, smiling. He was tall with an amused old-time face. He was a member of the FCAH board, though he'd never been elected. We'd all gone to the meeting, heard the speeches, and voted in the spring. The board had five members, including a treasurer, a secretary, and a chairperson. In the summer, we got an email saying a sixth member had been added, Ralph Rizzo, "who will bring his unique skills as a BMW salesman to the task of growing our program." Of course, Coach Ralph was really there to keep an eye on his son Brian, a happy eleven-year-old with dark curls spilling out of his helmet.

Many of the parents were new to hockey. The fathers had played football, which, because of all the research into head injuries, they'd judged too dangerous for their daughters and sons. Hockey seemed like a good alternative. Fast and exciting, here's a sport that's physical yet not quite as violent as football. There is hitting in hockey, but not until Bantam year, and even then it's not as frequent or as brutal as the tackling in football. It's possible to imagine a version of hockey that banishes checking altogether. Contact would be incidental, as in basketball, yet the game would remain essentially the same. Football is different. Football *is* hitting. The pigskin is like the McGuffin in a Hitchcock movie. It's there merely as an excuse—because the players need something to chase. Which explains the hockey boom. Whereas participation in Pop Warner football has fallen, participation in youth hockey has jumped. In 2019, close to 600,000 kids registered for travel hockey, a number that does not include the hundreds of thousands who play in house leagues.

The result is thousands of newbie parents. After much fieldwork, I am ready to break them into two categories. First, the big group, which I call "the clueless." They sign the forms, listen to the lectures, drive to the rinks, and cheer without really caring. They may arrive late or even step outside to take a business call in the middle of the action. These people are akin to old-time sports parents. They know this moment will pass, that, in the life of their child, hockey will be replaced first by something, then by something else. In the end, it's the passion and not the game that matters, so they don't get caught up in the particulars. The faces of these parents are calm and unbothered. That's not the case with the group in which I count myself: we are the crazies, the control freaks, the hyperinvolved, the nutters who have lost perspective. Yes, we are trying to relive our pasts. Yes, we are trying to acquire status through our children. But that's only part of it. To us, the game is more than a game. It's a metaphor. When it's not working, the world itself is not working. The ineffective coaches and favoritism represent the sort of bullshit that is ruining this country. It's the universal fix. It's the parent-coaches taking care of their own.

At times, it can seem as if the very concept of *team* has broken down. It's every man for himself.

In the course of a bad afternoon, such parents move from seat to seat in search of a perch from where life looks better. We know that luck is fickle, that everything changes. We can be recognized by the worry in our eyes. We are teeth grinders and restless sleepers. We suffer from tension headaches. We are shadow people between tournaments; we doze at the wheel on the way home. Our cars weave in traffic. We close our eyes when the whistle blows. If it looks like we are praying, it's because we are. We are asking God to shower our child with goals. I'd like to tell you what we look like or how we dress, but we are indistinguishable from other Americans. We come from every walk of life, every racial, economic, and ethnic background. We represent every sort of person and every sort of preference and go by every sort of pronoun. We check every box. We are they and me and him and her and you and them. We could be anyone, even the person in the next seat reading *Tom Sawyer*. We might be the woman you married, though neither you nor she will know it till halfway through that first season. You might be watching us from a distance and wondering, "What is wrong with that person?"

To you I say, "Don't judge. We mock what we are to become."

I was shocked when I first came down with symptoms. It started when Micah was a Squirt. There was a big play. He was in the middle of it. My heart began to race. Beads of sweat appeared on my forehead, though it was cold in the rink. My jaw tightened and I asked myself, "What is happening to me? Why am I freaking out?" Then, one day soon after, while watching my son score a goal, I experienced a paroxysm of joy. I'd felt nothing like it since college, and then only with the aid of stimulants. There is little to match the intoxication of seeing your child do something well. If you're a sports fan, you'll know the feeling. Have you ever watched your team— in my case, the Cubs—win a game on the last play? It's just like that, only your kid is the Cubs and you are everyone in the stands.

Some parents, not wanting to become a hockey asshole, bottle up their emotions instead. They say nothing when their kid scores, though you can see them trying to repress a grin. But most parents in the small group scream, the easiest way to exorcise the beast. They keep it positive though sound hysterical: "Let's go, Bears!" Some shout at their kids. It's praise from most: "Nice pass, Barry!" But criticism from others: "Where's your head, Patrick?" A few yell at the referee: "Get some glasses, zebra!" A handful taunt the opposition: "You suck, Ridgefield!" Some denounce their own team: "We suck!" Habits vary by region. This has to do with culture. People learn to heckle by watching their parents heckle. The mildest New Jersey heckler outdoes Connecticut's most vociferous. The nastiest are found on Long Island. No one can tell you exactly why. Maybe it's all the muscle shirts and cars up on blocks, or the gridlock on the L.I.E., or the proximity and distance of Manhattan. Maybe it's the grandparents—fathers teach daughters to heckle, daughters become mothers who teach their sons, who then have hockey-playing kids of their own. They do not merely heckle the other team on Long Island; they heckle the kids on the other team. A Garden City father called my son "a tiny piece of shit." A mother from Merrick wondered if all Ridgefield kids attend "fuckhead school."

When I was reporting my book *Monsters*, about the 1985

Chicago Bears, the quarterback Jim McMahon, whose kid played hockey in Northbrook, Illinois, told me about a father heckling his—McMahon's—son. Mac said the guy gave his kid the finger. Mac confronted him—this is the Punky QB we're talking about. The guy said, "I was giving the finger to another kid." He offered to apologize. Mac said, "No, you have to stand still as that kid gives *you* the finger—that's the only way this gets resolved."

There are occasionally fights in the stands, which is when youth hockey makes it into the newspapers. *The Toronto Star* likened a parent brawl at a rink outside Ontario to a "Tim Hortons commercial as directed by Quentin Tarantino." Reporting on a parent fight in another Canadian town, a writer from the *National Post* was shocked by what he found: "The picture that emerged was often sweet but often incredibly ugly, rife with tales of extra-marital affairs in rinky-dink hotels, fistfights in the stands, threats uttered, coaches bribed and dads getting so sloshed at tournaments that they wind up in the hospital while their child is fast asleep back at the hotel." In 2002, a hockey father named Thomas Junta beat another hockey father to death after a scrimmage in Massachusetts. In November 2014, Adam Proteau issued a plea in *The Hockey News*: "Whatever else you do for your kid during their time on the ice, do them a bigger service and ensure you're not one of the overbearing, interfering, egomaniacal embarrassments of hockey parents roaming arenas throughout North America."

At a Squirt game, one of our parents—a short, bespectacled dealer in rare books—got into it with a parent from Massapequa, who was all over our kids. The bookdealer shouted: "Hey, buddy. Why don't you yell at your kids, and we'll yell at ours?" Things escalated. The bookdealer was heading to the parking lot to fight the guy when I pulled him aside. "What's the best-case scenario?" I asked. "You beat up this asshole, get arrested, and go to jail. But let's be honest—that's probably not what's going to happen."

My father did not care about my hockey games. He came to only a few and did not pay attention when he did come. He yelled only one thing, and yelled it twice, once when I was seven and again when I was fifteen: "Get up! You're not hurt!"

But there's a new kind of hockey parent. Maybe it's what we got in place of the old American sense of mission. It's as if we're no longer one nation but a million little nations with a million little nationalisms, each being the project of turning a youth player into a star. Sports used to be seen as a hobby, a diversion. To many, it was considered a waste of time, like video games today. Now it's everything. That change is personified by two athletes, as known from the fables. First Lou Gehrig, the Yankees' "Iron Horse," who appeared in 2,130 consecutive Major League Baseball games. Gehrig's father, who'd emigrated from Germany, worked in a factory. He was epileptic and alcoholic. Gehrig's mother thought that Lou was the only hope for the future. She wanted him to study and go to college, but he only wanted to play baseball, so he'd sneak out. Gehrig became a star in spite of his upbringing. His mother was the old-model sports parent.

Elven Mantle, whom everyone called Mutt, was the new model. He'd been a semipro baseball player, good but not good enough. He was working in a lead and zinc mine in Oklahoma when his son Mickey—named after the Yankees catcher Mickey Cochrane—was born. Not making the majors was the big event in Mutt Mantle's life. He took that frustration and poured it into his son. He taught him how to throw, slide, and hit from both sides of the plate. He turned his boy into the specimen he'd never been. Mickey got off to a bad start in the majors. He did not get a hit in thirty-six at-bats and was sent down to the minors. It was Mickey's first failure, and he did not know what to do. He called his father and said he planned to quit. Mutt showed up ten hours later. He'd driven from Commerce, Oklahoma. He went to Mickey's closet and began packing his clothes.

"What are you doing?" Mickey asked.

"I'm taking you home," said Mutt. "I've got a job for you in the mine."

Which was exactly what Mickey needed—the threat of ordinary life. He was back in the majors by May. He became a Hall of Famer, but also an alcoholic. Pressure warped him. He had a great career and a troubled life. We've all got our kids in the Mutt Mantle training program now.

Scouting the opposition at Lake Placid,
New York

There were fifteen players on the Pee Wee A Bears. Imagine them being introduced like players in an NHL All-Star game, each skating out as an announcer calls their number and shares a few biographical details:

Number 19, Brian Rizzo! Brian was a rushing defenseman. He'd built his game, even if he didn't know it, in the style of Bobby Orr. Until the 1970s, even a good defenseman hardly ever scored. Bobby Orr changed that. He'd jump into the offensive rush. He could do this because he was a great skater, fast enough to get back on defense. By jumping into the offense, Orr put his team on an odd-man rush. In 1965, Jacques Laperrière, the Montreal Canadiens' All-Star defenseman, collected six goals and twenty-five assists. In 1974, Bobby Orr collected forty-six goals and eighty-nine assists. After 1977, every team in North America had a rushing defenseman. For the Pee Wee A Bears, it was Brian Rizzo, who'd been empowered by his father, Ralph Rizzo, one of our parent-coaches, to pick his spots. It gave his game an unpredictable, daredevil quality. Now and then, when Brian took off with the puck, you'd think, "Oh, God, here we go." The kid was a gambler. If things went well, it meant a dazzling scoring opportunity for the Bears. But if things went wrong, and they often did, it meant a dazzling scoring opportunity the other way. You did not look away when Brian was on the ice.

A rushing defenseman must be balanced by a stay-at-home defenseman who can cover both positions. A certain type of player excels at this. He or she tends to be sober and responsible, unconcerned with statistics or personal glory.

For the Bears, it was . . .

Number 12, Rick Stanley! Rick was lanky, loose-limbed,

the sort of skater who looks like he's taking his time even when he's flying. Kids loved him because he loved the game—he spent hours and hours in his driveway, working on his slap shot. He was dutiful and dedicated, which made sense when you got to know his father, Terry, a full-blown Deadhead and the Ridgefield Bears' only woke parent. Terry's Chevy Blazer was all social justice bumper stickers on the outside and all Jerry Garcia on the inside. Rick was often late to practice, for which he skated laps, though it was obviously Terry's fault.

We also had . . .

Number 32, Patrick Campi! Patrick was affectionate, always with his arm around a kid, bucking up the downtrodden, congratulating the scorers. His mom believed he belonged on Double A, and she was right. He was a fantastic athlete, and played the game with intuition. He always seemed to know what was going to happen on the ice. A handful of our players were in fact too good for the A team. They often got it wrong in the tryouts. Some believed it was corruption. Some believed it was intentionally done to balance the teams. Some believed it was simple incompetence. "You're over analyzing it," a father told me. "A lot of these coaches are just stupid." Because he was big, Patrick tended to draw excess attention from other teams. There's no checking till Bantam, which does not mean they don't hit, just that it draws a penalty. Never having had to deal with legal contact, Patrick had developed few survival skills. He skated blithely up the ice, head down, as if nothing could touch him. He'd already had two concussions.

"One more," the doctor told Campi's mother, "and he'll have to take up another sport."

"Like soccer?"

"Like badminton."

Then . . .

Number 64, Barry Meese, a.k.a. Moose! Our team was half first-year Pee Wees (ten- and eleven-year-olds) and half second-year Pee Wees (eleven- and twelve-year-olds). There can be a tremendous difference. A ten-year-old is usually prepubescent with downy cheeks. At twelve, the same kid might have become a mustachioed monster. Barry was a second-year Pee Wee, a big center with a hard shot. All he lacked was imagination. He'd do the same thing again and again: get the puck behind our net (good), skate in front of our own goalie (bad), carry the puck up the ice by himself (bad), make several players on the other team look silly (good), then lose the puck just inside the blue line (bad). And he did not pass. The only way to beat a faster team is by passing—you can pass faster than anyone can skate—but Barry wouldn't do it. I began to think of him as a devotee of a mystery cult whose only commandment was Thou Shalt Not Pass. When he did—I mean, yes, sometimes he did—it was always to his right. I wondered if he had a vision problem: Could it be as simple as that? I had a fantasy. I'd take him out to lunch, then bring him to Cohen's Fashion Optical, where he'd get tested, then fitted with frames, then bingo! He'd see the open wing, make the pass, get the pass, score!

Then . . .

Number 65, Leo Moriarty! A laid-back forward, he had flashes of brilliance followed by periods of indolence, when he seemed to lose focus. Maybe he was too happy, too cool. He showed up to the Winter Garden directly from lacrosse in shorts and flip-flops, which he called "slides," even when it was snowing. It pissed off Coach Hendrix. "Sandals at the rink? Just wait till someone steps on his foot with a skate and Leo loses a toe! Then we'll see how cool he looks."

Number 89, Roman Holian! He'd been adopted from an orphanage in Ukraine. Good hands, good wrists, but sensitive—a single word of criticism could undo him. He had snowy blond hair and myopic blue eyes that were corrected on the ice by goggles that made him look like a Martian. He was a scorer, but slow. He gummed up the rush.

Number 33, Becky Goodman! Her brothers were high school hockey stars, making her a kind of royalty. She'd grown up with the game, which is probably why she had a better feel for it than just about anyone. A stay-at-home defender, she was the biggest kid we had. When not in the locker room or in action, she was watching TikTok videos on her phone, studying dance moves. She had long blond hair and the glazed look of a screen addict. You'd never guess she was such a force on the ice.

Number 14, Joey McDermott! He was a skilled stick handler, and a constant scoring threat. He worked beautifully with his stepbrother Tommy—they communicated on a supersecret stepbrother frequency—but the coaches usually put Joey on defense. He was often in the company of his little brother Chase, a Squirt goalie. I sought Chase out at the rink because no one offered better postgame analysis. "He didn't score," Chase said after Campi missed an open net, "because deep down he doesn't want to score."

Number 15, Duffy Taylor! A wildly talented player, arguably the best Pee Wee in Ridgefield, Duffy had that single flaw—temper. He had the kind of blond hair that looks white in the sun, and his eyes were washed-out blue. He had ice vision, that rare thing—he could see the patterns and possibilities before anyone. He was a Double A talent placed on our roster by way of punishment, as a disobedient soldier might be transferred to the Aleutian Islands.

Number 66, "Broadway Jenny" Hendrix! Tiny, freckle-faced, incredibly hardworking, and show-tune singing, Broadway Jenny played forward on legs that went like pistons. You could almost hear them chugging. This was a girl getting fifteen pounds into a ten-pound sack, driven by a fuel even more powerful than love of the game—fear of her father, Coach Hendrix, who had taught her the sport. There was not a moment when Broadway Jenny did not know where she was supposed to be or what she was supposed to do on the ice. She would step out of the face-off to reposition her teammates before the puck was dropped. It was like having a coach in the game.

Number 55, "Broadway Julie" Sherman! A brown-haired, green-eyed, straight-A student, Broadway Julie was smart, modest, and happy just to find a place in the scheme. Why the nickname? Because her father was a well-known theatrical producer, many of whose plays had appeared on Broadway. Perhaps it was all the years of auditions that made him honest enough to describe his daughter as "a great kid but a third-line hockey talent. My heart wants her to lead," he told us, "but my head knows she belongs in the chorus."

Number 3, Jean Camus! He had the name of a Quebecois, a French-Canadian icebound maestro, but he asked teammates to call him Jack. If they called him Jean, which they often did, he flew into a rage. Now and then, he'd do something great, made thrilling by its rarity. He loved skating but only liked hockey.

Number 00, Dan Arcus! Our goalie, "the Arc," turned out

to be the key to whatever success we had. He was big and quiet, like his father. For Jocko, it was the Dodge Charger that did the talking. For Dan, it was that goalie stick and oversize pads. Having the Arc in the net was like having an ace on the mound every night.

And then my own kid . . .

Number 45, Micah Cohen! When Micah made his first travel team, we were told to choose a number for his jersey. This is important. We're all numerologists now. It seemed best to take a number that had belonged to an NHL great—such a number is blessed. He tried 9, which had belonged to Gordie Howe; 99, which had belonged to Wayne Gretzky; 11, which had belonged to Mark Messier. They were all taken. He went after a few others—7 (Phil Esposito), 21 (Stan Mikita), 87 (Sidney Crosby). Taken, taken, taken. He switched to the numbers of football players, because, as I explained, it's the spirit and not the particular sport that matters. He settled on 45, which had been worn by Chicago Bears' safety Gary Fencik, a.k.a. "the Hitman." Fencik was a legendary over-achiever, a medium-size athlete who got by on smarts. He played at Yale, was drafted and cut by the Dolphins, then walked on in Chicago, where he stuck around for fourteen seasons, becoming an All-Pro and the Bears' career intercep-tion leader. Fencik was never the best player on any of his teams, not even in high school. He just kept improving. In him I recognized Micah, who starts at the bottom of each new roster and climbs. Sometimes I think it's the way he skates. There's a hitch in Micah's stride. He's fast but not pretty. He does not look like the kid in the instructional video. As some players overachieve in tryouts, he underachieves. He can't skate the cones and doesn't nail the drills. All he can do is play hockey.

The Pee Wee A Bears had a Bad News Bears quality. We'd become a dumping ground for good players with an attitude problem, for disobedient, uncoachable kids with an interest in e-cigarettes and curse words, Double A players held back in hopes of reform. The experience of being relegated was supposed to teach them humility, but it only pissed them off. That was the edge, the chip on the shoulder of half the Single A Pee Wees. The key player—our version of Kelly Leak, the minibike-riding thug who made the Bad News Bears formidable—was our short, foulmouthed, towheaded center . . .

Number 4, Tommy McDermott! The oldest and smallest kid on the team, he moved less like a North American player than like a European—all dipsy-doodle stick-handling, toe-dragging finesse. He'd forsake the easy way, preferring the fun of making some kid look clumsy, slow, and stupid. If Tommy were a painter, you'd call him baroque. If he were a living room, you'd call him busy. He was a classic small-town bad kid, always in trouble at the rink and at school. Caught vaping. Overheard telling racist, anti-Semitic jokes.

On the way home from practice, Micah would speak of words and phrases that he'd learned from Tommy McDermott.

"Like what?" I asked one day.

"I can't tell you."

"Please. Just one."

"OK. 'Beat my meat.'"

"What else?"

"'Blow job.'"

A parent complained to the board. "I knew my son would eventually learn these things," she said, "but I was hoping for a few more years of innocence."

When Tommy told racist or anti-Semitic jokes, he did not seem to know what he was saying. He delivered them as you might deliver a box. *Here it is.* After a particularly tasteless example led to a brawl, Coach Pete sent an email to the team:

> Subject: Respect and teamwork
>
> All: It has come to my attention that there had been some inappropriate behavior in the locker room. This is disappointing, especially after such a good start to the season, with strong team camaraderie. As always, my job as a coach is to guide our team on the ice, at practice and at games, but it's also my job to demonstrate to the kids what it means to be a team player. I hope you will join me in reminding our players of the value of respect of the game, coaches, players, and others on and off the ice. This is an integral part of our ability to work together as a team, as well as coexist in our hockey community. My hope is that from this day, we will uplift and support each other as we grow as a team.
>
> Coach Pete

Tommy was no different from half the kids I grew up with—a good kid having a hard time. Two sets of parents, divorce, etc. He gave the Pee Wee A Bears an attitude. The

Double A team was like the 1996 New York Yankees, squeaky clean in suits and ties, thanking coaches and mothers. We were more like the 1975 Oakland Raiders, scalawags in flips-flops and T-shirts, believing in only one thing: just win, baby! From the start, our kids had a single goal: catch and beat the Double As.

SEPTEMBER

The first cold nights. The leaves on the maple trees began to turn, gold at the tips, red at the stems. They didn't know they were dying. The grass was stiff when the school bus came, and there was woodsmoke at night, football weather, bonfires, cheerleaders, and homecoming. Each day was shorter than the last. The best were indistinguishable from the best days of spring, yet the opposite. April afternoons portend the coming of summer, while September leads to winter, when everything is sheathed in ice. In one case, you're ascending. In the other, you're falling. There'd be no way to survive it without hockey.

The Pee Wee A Bears had their first game just after Labor Day. We were in the NMHL, the Nutmeg Hockey League, which meant we played two games a weekend, one home, one away. Including tournaments, the kids would have fifty games before the season was over. Every NMHL team is ranked on opening day. Rankings are based on the organization's previous performance, self-appraisal, and whatever else goes into the all-powerful algorithm. About eighty teams are ranked. Those that finish in the top twenty play for the Tier 2 championship. The next twenty play for the Tier 3 championship.

(Tier 1 is Triple A.) The Double As began the season ranked fifteenth. The Single As began ranked fifty-second. In order to catch the Double As, the Pee Wee As would have to climb. You did this by beating top teams or at least staying close. Better to lose a tight one to a top team than to squeak by a cellar-dweller. Coach Pete didn't even want to play any team ranked more than ten spots behind us. If a team was ranked in the bottom half of the NMHL, you could beat them and still lose position. The reverse was also true. In other words, you could lose by winning and win by losing.

The games were booked by Alan Hendrix, a parent-coach and also our scheduler. It was a hugely important position. During the hockey season, the scheduler has more effect on your life than any spouse or boss. A brilliant scheduler means a glide through the fall and into spring, a rise from darkness to light. A bad scheduler sets your kids up for humiliation and sets you up for early mornings, long drives, and lack of sleep. Micah's Squirt scheduler had sent us to every corner of the state yet never attended games. Her husband went instead. We joked that she must be having an affair.

Coach Hendrix was a terrific scheduler. Every game was booked with the algorithm in mind. No goal would be wasted. We started at home against the Enfield Eagles. The Winter Garden is one of the smallest rinks in the NMHL. No concession stand. No coffee machine. Just ice, boards, Plexiglas, bleachers, locker rooms. You'd never guess such a place could be the site of so much drama. In an age of huge facilities—at the Palisades Center Mall, we played beside a bowling alley—the Winter Garden was a wonderful throwback. It was Wrigley Field or Fenway Park, a lyric little bandbox.

Pee Wee kids carry their own bags, sticks, and jerseys, laundered and toted on wooden hangers, like tuxedos for a prom. They dressed in silence before that first game, nervous. That's a pleasure of any sport—the accumulation and relief of stress. Until the puck is dropped, you're not sure you'll remember how to do anything. Your only thought is *Don't screw up!* Coach Pete was wearing a black jacket, jeans, and Vans. His hair was swept back, and you could see razor burn above his collar. The parents waited in the bleachers, as nervous as the kids. I know I was. I kept thinking to myself that Micah barely made this team; he was the last player selected, which should make him the worst kid on the ice. I wondered if the evaluators had been right in the first place. Maybe he did belong in the lower group.

The Pee Wee A Bears were an odd mix of speed and grit. It did not take long to see that they had something special. The kids zipped the puck all over the ice in that first period, and scored, but took their time doing it, as if savoring. In this world, style can be as important as skill. Every kid contributed. They cheered one another and fist-bumped on the bench. They hooted, "Arc, Arc, Arc," for their goalie. The feeling among the parents was *Someone made a mistake; this team is way better than it should be.*

Coach Pete played three lines. Tommy McDermott centered the first, with Patrick Campi on one wing and Broadway Jenny Hendrix on the other. Barry Meese centered the second, with Leo Moriarty on one wing and Jean "Jack" Camus on the other. Duffy Taylor centered the third, with Broadway Julie Sherman on one wing and Micah on the other. We had two defensive units: Brian Rizzo and Joey McDermott; Rick

Stanley and Becky Goodman. Becky, fast and smart, often had to cover for Rick, who was slow but tough. He was dangerous in the way of a jellyfish. He could hurt you, but only if you stepped on him. Roman Holian, a big, blond right wing who now and then missed a practice or even a game to attend Ukrainian Camp, sat out most of the first game. Roman had improved greatly since tryouts—kids grow over the summer—but Coach Pete, working off a dated depth chart, hardly noticed.

Micah had played center his previous seasons. He had to learn wing, which would take time. He kept drifting to the middle of the ice—that was a problem. And the game was indeed faster, the players better, but that turned out to be good. In such a case, you either fail or adjust. It took a few shifts, but he adjusted.

He got his first scoring chance at the end of the period. We were already winning 2–1. Tommy had deflected a shot taken by Brian; Barry had banged a rebound in from the crease, the area immediately in front of the goal that's shaded blue and bordered with a red line and that belongs to the goalie. (An opposing player cannot precede a puck into the crease.) Duffy was battling for possession along the boards. The puck popped out of the scrum. Micah got it and went up ice. He was skating beside Broadway Julie. He crossed the blue line, turned, and passed to Duffy, who was coming in late. Duffy faked to Broadway Julie but passed to Micah, who went behind the net and passed to Broadway Julie, who sent it back to Duffy, who lasered the puck cross-ice to Micah, who flipped it over the Enfield goalie's shoulder into the net.

A characteristic post-goal celebration

That first goal was crucial for Micah's season. It told him he belonged.

The game flowed back and forth from there. Tommy dominated with speed, and tremendous acceleration. The puck was a yo-yo that kept returning to his stick. Early in the third period, he passed to Jack Camus, who was fifteen feet from the net. An Enfield defender skated at Jack, who blanched, then threw the puck into the corner. His brain could not forget those concussions. The best players have a bad memory. Like dogs, they remember only the good times. Jack was too smart for the game.

Coach Pete waved Jack to the bench. Broadway Jenny hopped onto the ice. She swarmed the Enfield goalie like a paparazzo, softening the scene for everyone, including Patrick Campi, who broke a 3–3 tie with a blast from ten feet inside the blue line.

Micah scored again a few minutes later. Our forwards had

peppered Enfield with every kind of shot, but their goalie was solid. Micah had taken two runs. In the first, he went behind the net and shot the puck from the far side—the standard hockey wraparound. Goalies are usually prepared for it. As soon as a forward goes back there, the goalie slides to cover the far post. Micah's second attempt was like the first. He got the puck and went around the net and again attempted a wraparound, this time trying to jam it in with force. But the goalie was strong. He not only stopped Micah but sent him sprawling. Micah began to make what looked like the same failed maneuver, only this time stopped halfway behind the net and skated back, catching the goalie out of position. He slid the puck in for his second goal.

Meanwhile, the parents: Jerry Sherman was cheering, Sue Campi was toasting with her third beer of the day, and Parky Taylor was banging on the glass, shouting at Duffy. Jocko Arcus was standing behind the goal and moving his arms, as if controlling his son Dan with strings.

When the final horn sounded, it was Bears 5, Eagles 3. Nothing better than starting the season with a win. The Ridgefield parents gossiped in the lobby as their kids changed. Many of us already had visions of glory. Coach Pete came out and stood with us. He was happy, too. He knew we had a good group. In such a case, he said, a big part of the coach's job is to simply step aside and let the kids play.

Pop Warner football starts in August and is done by Thanksgiving. Little League baseball starts in April and wraps up in time for summer vacation. Youth hockey goes on and on. It's an endurance test, an expression of time. It carries through three of the four seasons, sees the coming and going of autumn and winter and spring, the falling and returning of leaves. A player might start as a boy, have his first wet dream in a hotel room at an October showcase, be interested in girls by Christmas, and emerge from the state tournament as a man. The length of the calendar means ups and downs, streaks and slumps, stretches of excitement followed by longueurs in which the wind dies and the ship stalls in the doldrums.

In mid-September, the Bears were 5 and 0. We'd beaten the Greenwich Skating Club and the Greenwich Wings, the Bedford Bears and the New Rochelle Lightning. By the end of the month, the proclivities and mannerisms of each player had been revealed. Becky Goodman, our biggest player, blond hair cascading down, eyes fixed on the advancing forward as she glided backward toward our net, was the best defender, a rock-solid presence who could be beat but not outplayed. Tommy McDermott, our first-line center, was the principal scoring threat—now and then he'd go end-to-end. Barry Meese—"Moose!"—our second-line center, often seemed like he was about to score, then didn't. Philosophical question: What happens to all the beautiful plays that leave no mark in the record books, the double moves that end with a puck rattling off the post? Barry led the team in that invisible category—the most almost-goals, the most almost-assists. Roman Holian found a way to contribute. He had a knack for finishing. He'd jump into the Plexiglas behind the goal when he scored and shout, "*Tak!*" which, according to Micah, means "Yes!" in Ukrainian.

A handful of early-season moments stand out. Joey Mc-Dermott intercepting a pass in our zone, putting a puck off the boards onto Leo's stick, Leo head-manning it to Barry, whose shot turns into a rebound, which Jack Camus buries. Rick Stanley, our tall, quiet, dutiful defenseman, scoring with a floater from the blue line. Our goalie Dan Arcus dropping into a split as he reaches up to snag a puck out of the air.

The Pee Wee A Bears overperformed. We were a third-tier team that, with the just-right mix of players on the ice, could turn a close game into a route with a deluge of goals. The hockey played at such times was wide open and free, unsound and fun to watch. Between-the-legs passes, off-the-glass passes, from-behind-the-net passes and shots, boomers off the pass—known as one-timers—slap shots from the point. It was a highlight reel when it worked, but not everyone approved. When the team switched into high gear, some kids faded. You had to be fast to play this way—and creative. You had to forget a lot of what you'd been taught. It was the hockey version of playground basketball. Barry Meese, Patrick Campi, Broadway Jenny Hendrix, Broadway Julie Sherman, Roman Holian, Jack Camus—none of them could keep up when things really got going.

Coach Pete was fine with it, because it worked. But it soon became clear that Coach Hendrix hated it. Even when we were winning, he said we were winning "like idiots, stupid and ugly."

"There's a right way to play this game and a wrong way," he explained. "This is the wrong way. It will not work against top teams. It's elitist and excludes half our players. We need to play team hockey—good, solid, sound, textbook team hockey that includes everyone."

I thought his beef was really about his daughter Broadway Jenny. She was a dutiful player—hard work, no magic. She could not keep up with the top skaters when they started blazing. Coach Hendrix wanted the team to adhere to a style more amenable to Broadway Jenny's talent. She was supposed to be a leader but became a bit player at such times, watching a handful of ne'er-do-wells turn the game into a skills competition. They'd score, they'd win, they'd crank the music in the locker room. After each victory, one of the kids—usually Tommy or Duffy—would vow to catch and thrash the Double As, "those flexing try-hards!"

The rest of September was a wash of color, vibrant and indistinct. It's not the games I remember. It's the blur—the excitement, stresses, and satisfactions of a hockey parent. In my mind, it's always early morning. I'm waking Micah in the dark, carrying his bag and jerseys to the car, closing the trunk softly so as not to wake the rest of the family. We are the only car on the road. Micah sleeps in back as I search the radio for anything but politics. The sun comes up, revealing green New England. We join a handful of Jeeps and Hondas on the interstate. I am convinced that each of these cars carries a hockey player and a mother or father en route to a game. You see them bleary-eyed at Dunkin' Donuts. The kids nod to each other, but the fathers look away, convinced of their solitude, believing they are unique and not in fact part of a demographic, living one version of a life that's being lived by millions of others.

It's not the towns I remember, nor the faded industrial

cities. It's the rinks, which, taken together, form a web that spans the entire region. The Sono Ice House in Norwalk. The Northford Ice Pavilion. Bennett Rink in West Haven. And the prep school rinks: Taft, Brunswick, Kent, The Gunnery in Washington, Connecticut. The walls are papered with ancient team photos: 1935, 1926, 1918. You could spend an afternoon studying the faces in these pictures, as redolent of a lost world as a wooden hockey stick. Zagat should publish a guide with each facility ranked and reviewed. It'd be good to be forewarned about the coldness of The Gunnery, or told where to get a decent cup of coffee near the Twin Rinks in Stamford.

The kids hang their jerseys from hooks, drop their bags, head for "dryland training"—jump, stretch, run the bleachers—then get dressed. There's music in the locker room. It's meant to launch the kids onto the ice like bullets from a gun. The task of assembling the playlists and hauling around the speakers tends to fall to a self-appointed player. For the Pee Wee A Bears, it was Brian Rizzo, who, in addition to classic hockey hair, had classic hockey-music taste. He blasted the same songs that my teams listened to in the 1980s: "Walk This Way," "It's Tricky," "Welcome to the Jungle." Coach Pete talks to the team before each game as Coaches Rizzo and Hendrix lean against the wall, nodding. Some kids devour these speeches; others, like Tommy McDermott, try not to laugh.

Over time, the proclivities of the parents become as clear as those of their kids. Most of them watch the games with other parents from the bleachers, but a few sit by themselves. Jerry Sherman can't tolerate a crowd when his daughter Broadway Julie is on the ice. He stands at the far end with one or two handpicked confidants. He does not want to be over-heard talking smack about coaches or kids.

Some parents watch only from ice level, while others sit up high, as if assuming the vantage of God. Judd Meese sat by himself in the top row of the bleachers. Jocko and Camille Arcus set up behind the goal. When the teams switched sides between periods, so did they. You could chart their position as you chart the phases of the moon. Becky Goodman's mother, Roz, waited in the car—she said she couldn't stand to watch. Now and then, her husband, Bill, would go out with a cup of coffee and an update. Duffy's father, Parky, watched from the corner. "It's the only spot that lets you see the entire ice without turning your head," he explained. I like to watch from the offensive zone.

Some parents dressed for games in business casual, but most wore gear, Bears hats and Bears sweatshirts. Some mothers—hockey moms—had pins that showed their child in action. In the way of a high school girlfriend, Sue Campi wore one of her son's old jerseys to the games.

The parents convened in the lobby after the final horn to wait. The girls seemed to change faster than the boys. They were in street clothes before the boys had taken off their skates. The coach exited next, avoiding eye contact as he headed to his car. He'd wave off anyone who tried to stop him, saying, "Twenty-four-hour rule." Then came most of the boys, nodding and accepting congratulations. A half hour after the rest had changed, the stragglers emerged, three or four kids who took forever. Micah was always among them, usually accompanied by Joey and Tommy McDermott.

The drive home is a melancholy mood. Dark roads, towns

in the distance. Best is when you come upon your own house in an unusual way, as if by accident. You don't recognize it at first. You sit confused, appreciating your life as you appreciate a thing that belongs to someone else.

The Bears had their first really physical game in late September in Northford, Connecticut, a few miles outside New Haven. To get there, you take the Merritt Parkway, a beautiful highway built in the 1930s, the age of the Chrysler Imperial. Ten minutes from Northford, the Merritt goes beneath a small green mountain. That tunnel marks the transition from Fairfield County to the rest of the world. Before it, lush suburbia. Beyond it, smokestacks and factories. The Bulldogs wear Yale jerseys, but are in no way affiliated with the school. After games in Northford, Ridgefield parents often talk of writing a letter to the president of the university: "Dear Mr. Salovey, do you know what sort of sportsmanship is being practiced in your name?"

Before warm-ups, our parents stood along the boards examining the Northford players: *No way that kid is under fifteen!* Parky made the usual joke about grabbing a beer with one of the Bulldogs. A debate ensued: Are the Northford kids big, or are the Ridgefield kids small? We split fifty-fifty on the question. "It has nothing to do with DNA," Sue Campi said. "It's nurture, not nature. There's no McDonald's in Ridgefield. Northford has two. And a Burger King. And a Popeyes, Dairy Queen, and Wendy's. Fast food. That's the difference. The hormones in the meat trigger puberty at age nine or ten. Demand birth certificates and you'll see. According to the calendar, these kids are kids, but when it comes to biology, they could be serving in the army."

Parky had a different theory. "I've been through the tunnel enough to know what they're doing," he said. "Their best players are always their smallest, and the biggest can never skate. Isn't it obvious? The Bantams who don't make travel play in Pee Wee, and the Pee Wees who don't make travel play in Squirt."

When an especially big Bulldog waddled out of the locker room, Terry Stanley whistled through his teeth. It was the sort of whistle you hear on the observation deck of the Hoover Dam.

"Look at him!" said Sharon Rizzo. "Why should our kids even play this game? They're gonna get creamed."

This made me think of Exodus, when Moses, knowing the freed slaves will have to battle their way into Canaan, sends ahead some scouts. They return with an alarming report. Converted into hockey-parent vernacular, it'd go like this: "Look at them! No way those kids are under fifteen! Maybe they can lend us their razors! Why even play this game?" God condemns the Hebrews to forty years in the wilderness. This is Jehovah as a hockey coach, blowing his whistle. The Hebrews do not have the courage to fight so must wander until those born as slaves die. What Sharon Rizzo said wasn't even true. In hockey, size is no match for speed, skill, intelligence. As long as we played fast and smart, we'd be fine, but some of our players overheard Sharon. Kids are suggestible. If you tell them they don't have a chance, they don't.

Tommy McDermott lined up against the Northford center—Meacham, number 88—for the opening face-off. It was one of those funny disparities you get in youth sports: tiny versus massive; kale versus Big Mac. It began just as you'd expect. Meacham sent Tommy reeling, took the puck, and plowed ahead. The parents quickly gathered into enemy camps: home and away, us and them. Insults were exchanged, but it was mostly them insulting us. It was a culture clash. Before the game, a stranger warned me: "Be careful—these people are insane."

The Ridgefield parents, players, and coaches were soon mad at the referees. I've told Micah this is silly, that the refs have nothing against his team, that they don't care who wins. "The idea that they choose a side is idiotic," I said, though that's not always what I believe. In Northford, the refs did indeed seem to let the home team get away with a lot. If they did not call roughing or tripping, then size really would be the only thing that mattered. Northford's first goal came halfway through the opening period. A Northford defenseman uncorked a slap shot from the blue line. It hit Dan Arcus in the face mask. You could hear the clank across the rink. He stumbled. Players from both teams fought for the rebound. As Dan reached for the puck, that big Meacham kid knocked him down. Another Northford player then shot the puck into the empty net. Goal. Horn. Bedlam. Only it shouldn't have counted. The goalie had been interfered with, which, instead of a goal, should have meant a two-minute penalty on them.

How had the ref missed it?

Coach Pete called a time-out. I could not hear him, but I knew what he'd be saying: "Don't let them take you out of your game. Fight back, but keep it clean. Don't get angry. It's what they want. Just win, baby."

Some of our kids responded appropriately. Leo fought for position in front of the net. Barry lowered his shoulder into a kid trying to take him out. Becky cleared their forwards away from our crease. But others acted inappropriately. Duffy lost his head completely. By the end of the first period, he was reeling around like a popped balloon, a drunk looking for a fight. Coach Pete scolded him. Coaches Rizzo and Hendrix admonished him. He didn't care. To play with edge means convincing yourself the kids on the other team are not merely trying to win but trying to annihilate you. It feels personal. Duffy was like a frontier sheriff who becomes a bigger threat to the town than the bad guys. He had that righteous hockey thing, only too much of it. The job of a coach is to recognize and redirect such energy, make it clear to a kid like Duffy that scoring is the only revenge. If this point was ever going to be made, here was a perfect opportunity. That way, even if we lost—we were going to lose—a positive would come out of it. But that's not what happened. Duffy instead went from cursing to shoving, from shoving to hitting. Coach Pete should've sat him down and told him to cool off, but simply let him play until the inevitable happened. It came at the end of the first. Three players were battling in the corner, Meacham among them. You could see that big number 88 hunched over, head a foot from the boards. Flying from the blue line, Duffy hit Meacham in the back, launching him into the corner, where he crumbled, then lay inert. The ref blew his whistle, skated over, and looked down. He motioned to the Northford bench. Parents on both sides got quiet. The kids on the ice took a knee, as they'd been taught. A Bulldogs coach shuffled out in Timberlands.

What Duffy did is called boarding—when you hit a defenseless player, a player who can't see you coming, into the boards from behind. It's among the worst penalties in hockey because it's among the most dangerous. That's how kids are paralyzed. Everyone applauded when Meacham finally stood. He missed the next shift but was back in the second period, playing as rough and dirty as before. Which was not the point. Duffy had transgressed—that was the point. He was heaped in shame and driven out, ejected from the game. He skated away slowly, sadly, then reappeared beside his father in street clothes, looking surprisingly harmless and small.

The Bears were given a "two and ten" penalty. For two minutes, we'd have only three players to face their five. One of our kids would have to sit in the box for two minutes, and another would have to sit for ten. Coach Hendrix called for Roman and Micah, waving them into the cooler. Roman would sit for two, Micah for ten. The shame of serving another man's sentence! The injustice! Had we really traveled all this way for Micah to miss nearly a third of the game? It infuriated me. I tried to hide my emotions—someone had to serve the penalty, after all—but I had a hard time doing it.

Northford scored on the power play, then scored again, then again. It had been 1–0 when Micah went into the box. It was 4–0 when he came out. It was 8–1 at the end of the game, a serious blow to the algorithm. Our players consoled their goalie, Dan Arcus, then went listlessly through the handshake line. Some of the Northford kids, instead of saying "Good game" as they shook hands—that's the custom—said, "Good scoreboard," which led to pushing and shoving.

The Ridgefield parents gathered in the lobby to commiserate. I've been in the Chicago Cubs locker room after the team's eighth straight loss. This was even worse. Anger. Confusion. Depression. Everyone wanted an explanation. Was it Duffy's fault? Did Coach Pete fail us? Do we need to put our kids on a starch-heavy diet? Or maybe we just had to get that one serious thumping out of the way.

I asked Coach Hendrix what he thought, but wish I hadn't. He had only bad things to say about our team and our players and our style. He spoke with terrific intensity. His face turned red, his words came faster and faster.

"It's only one game," I reminded him.

"Don't give me that," he said. "We've been getting by on individual play. We've now hit the wall. If we continue to play like this, we will lose and lose and lose."

When I asked about Duffy's penalty, he cursed and said, "He's a bad kid."

"You've got to channel his energy," I said. "You can teach him."

"Teach him what?" said Coach Hendrix. "How to be a good person? If his parents can't teach him right from wrong, how can I?"

Broadway Jenny was at her father's side, head down. Grace Hendrix was on the phone a few feet away, keeping an eye on everything. I complimented Broadway Jenny on her hustle. She looked up and smiled, but her eyes were bloodshot.

"You want to meet us at Dairy Queen?" I asked.

Coach Hendrix snorted.

"No thanks," he said. "We're going to Newington."

"Why Newington?"

"We play them next week. We're going to scout."

"Scout?"

It was the first I'd heard about Coach Hendrix's scouting. He'd apparently been traveling all over Connecticut to check out each team we'd play. He was the strange adult sitting alone in the bleachers. "Does anyone know who that man is?"

He'd write the name and number of every ten- and eleven-year-old in his notebook beside evaluations of speed, style, shot, and demeanor, strengths and weaknesses. He might go back to see the same team two or three times, even if it meant crisscrossing the state. If he could not attend in person, he'd watch the game on one of the apps—LiveBarn, HockeyTV—that stream from various rinks, freezing on particular plays, watching them again and again. He'd then brief Coach Pete. "This kid is good, but he can't take pressure," he might say. "If we get someone to chirp at him—Duffy? Tommy?—it'll wreck him."

Parky and his son Duffy were at Dairy Queen when Micah and I arrived. Duffy was drinking a shake. Parky was eating a Blizzard. The boarding penalty, the ejection—it had been a stressful afternoon for Parky, who, like millions of Americans, self-medicated with food. He would put on at least ten pounds in the course of the season.

Micah talked about the officiating all the way home.

"Cahoots" is the word he used.

"That ref was in cahoots."

"Why would the ref care who wins?" I asked.

"It was a Northford ref," Micah explained. "A home-towner!"

"Don't make accusations without evidence," I said.

"I do have evidence," he said, hair damp, eyes shining.

"Fine. Let's hear it."

"The ref got confused and skated to the Northford bench and asked, 'What period is this?' And one of their kids said, 'It's the third period, Dad.'"

I had trouble calming down when I got home. The violence of the thrashing and the anger of Coach Hendrix stayed with me. I texted a handful of parents, who, in their return texts, revealed themselves to be equally irritated. This marked the beginning of the postgame exchanges that would keep me company through the season. I texted with Duffy's father, Parky Taylor; Patrick's mother, Sue Campi; and Barry's father, Judd Meese. But it was Broadway Julie's father, Jerry Sherman, who became my hockey confidant.

> From Rich Cohen to Jerry Sherman, September 28, 9:33 p.m.:
>
> RC: Such bullshit. The playing time is all out of whack. Should I say something to the coaches?
>
> JS: Saying anything to these guys will be like peeing into the wind.
>
> RC: Well, I've been known to empty my bladder into a nor'easter.
>
> RC: Hey, I just tried to call you.
>
> JS: Sorry, I was getting lectured.
>
> RC: By who?
>
> JS: My wife. Seems I've been too loud at games. Do you think Barry's father heard me? I'm sorry, but that fucking kid doesn't pass! And the lines! I get situational hockey. I don't get playing favorites. Hendrix's kid played 38 minutes! My Julie had two shifts under 20 seconds. My fear is that we are the only people who see it. I know Hendrix and Rizzo know it. I think Rizzo does what he's told, and Coach Pete is intimidated. I get it, those parents are assistant coaches,

but Hendrix's kid being on the ice for the final
3 minutes and no one else getting out is horseshit.

RC: Intimidated by who?

JS: Hendrix. You've got a 25-year-old coach and a
50-year-old insane parent screaming on the bench. I
feel sorry for Coach Pete.

OCTOBER

Autumn really begins in October. The hills look like a fire in the distance, the wind blows and the branches sway and the leaves drift down and you say to yourself, "So this is why they call it 'fall.'" Everything is dropping, drifting, *falling*. It's the world preparing for sleep. God will soon hammer a lid over the sky. Most years, it happens slowly. Each day is a little shorter, bleaker, darker. You don't even notice until someone points it out. Or it can come in the course of a night. You go to sleep in the summer. You wake up and it's fall. The leaves have turned. You drive beneath a golden canopy. The lights in the stores come on early. The cakes glimmer in the windows of the gluten-free bakeries.

It turned out to be a complicated month for the Pee Wee A Bears, Micah, and me. What started in freewheeling, high-scoring joy was grinding into something else. Micah worked his way up to the first line by the fourth week of the season, which meant skating with better players and getting more ice time. It had only been a few games, but he was having success with Tommy at center and Leo on right wing. Though scoring and creating plays, Micah was also struggling with his new role as a wing. He was often out of position, too deep in his own zone or caught offside. He could not deal with any kind of double team. I told him he needed to create space. When he asked how, I showed him clips of the Blackhawks' Patrick Kane deploying my favorite decoy: the fake slap shot. "You wind up like you're going to blast one," I explained. "It freezes the defense, same as a pump fake in football. Then gather the puck and skate around. It works every time." I did not know if Micah was even paying attention, but sure enough, in the third period of the next game, with two defensemen closing, he faked a slap shot. The players froze. Micah went around and scored. It was a special moment, because, for the most part, no one ever listens to me.

The Pee Wee A Bears had their first "showcase" game—this is when they get looked at by prep coaches; none of our kids were ever recruited—at the Berkshire School in Sheffield, Massachusetts, which is two hours north of the Winter Garden. You take the Taconic State Parkway, which winds through the foothills of America's oldest mountains. There's a tattoo parlor in every town, a donut shop and CBD dispensary. Iron bridges cross the cold streams. The Berkshire School is beautiful, a jewel centered by an NHL-quality ice facility. It was *too* nice. The glory and big-time nature of it intimidated our team. You wanted Coach Pete to go out on the ice with a tape measure and show the kids that the distances were all the same as those back in Ridgefield, but that was not his style.

The game was an obvious mismatch from the start. Every player on the Berkshire Rattlers was better than every player on the Bears. I later learned that Coach Hendrix expected us to lose badly. He'd scheduled the game as a "wake-up call." He wanted to cut "the hotshots down to size." The Rattlers were not only more skilled but also better coached. They knew their positions and ran set plays. They knew how to break out of their zone, trap our puck carriers, run a power play, and kill a penalty. Here were fifteen kids working in concert, beating us individually and also beating us as a group. Coach Hendrix scheduled the game to reveal the flaws in our players, but he had also revealed the flaws in our coaches. Late in the first period, the Rattlers executed something like the backyard-football hook-and-ladder play. Their center passed to their left wing, who'd positioned himself along the boards at the red line. Instead of controlling the puck, the left wing deflected it to the right wing, who was sprinting up ice. Duffy, having chased the puck, was left behind. It made him look slow and foolish, like a dog chasing a toy that's yanked away. Embarrassed and frustrated, Duffy lashed out. He knocked down the biggest Berkshire kid and became a human pincushion as a result, checked and tripped by every Rattler. They chirped at him. He called them "F-tards," a construction I've heard nowhere else.

Leo's father, Albert, was disgusted.

"Why don't we use a time-out?" he asked.

"Because these idiots don't know what they're doing," said Sue Campi.

Coach Pete did call a time-out, but it didn't help. We simply could not score. Tommy made a good move late in the second and actually got a hard shot on net. The goalie made the save, then said something to Micah, who'd come in for a rebound. Micah responded. (He'd never tell me what he said, but it must have been bad.) Another kid shoved Micah from behind. His legs went out and he fell straight back, hitting his head on the ice. He lay motionless. Coach Rizzo went out to check, then waved over Coach Hendrix, who waved over Coach Pete.

"A three-coach injury!" said Jerry Sherman, shaking his head.

"Get up," I yelled, channeling my father. "You're not hurt!"

"But what if he is hurt?" I asked myself. "What if he's badly hurt?"

Such moments are clarifying. They make you know that all your previous obsessions and worries were pointless, stupid. Micah's health is the only thing that matters. Spending time together—drives to and from the games, late-night talks—that's what it's all about. The rest is meaningless.

How did I forget?

But Micah looked OK when he got up and skated to the bench. I expected him to be on for his next shift. I wanted him to finish strong. Play the last minute with the same intensity as you played the first. Play when you're getting crushed the same as when the game is tied. That's the key. But he took off his helmet and sat down. Even from a distance, he looked dazed. Here's what I was thinking as I made my descent from the bleachers: that part of my life, the part when Micah and I drive and talk and stop for dinner, was over, and now began the part in which I lifted him into and out of his special chair.

Micah was talking to Coach Hendrix when I got to the bench but not looking at him. He was gazing deeply into nothing. He did not appear to be hurt or even unhappy. He simply seemed adrift.

Coach Hendrix pulled me aside and said, "He failed the concussion test."

"What's the concussion test?"

"We ask questions, things they should know. Micah couldn't answer any of them."

"What'd you ask him?"

"I asked him your wife's mother's maiden name. He couldn't tell me."

"I couldn't tell you. What else?"

"I asked him where you and your wife had your first date."

"We didn't have a first date," I said. "We met at a Super Bowl party."

I sat next to Micah and checked him out myself. I asked how he felt. He said he felt fine. I then gave him my own concussion test, cobbled together from movies. I asked if he knew where he was. He did. I asked if he could tell me the day of the week and the time of day. He was close enough. I asked him his name, the names of his brothers, his birthday. He got them all.

I asked him if he wanted to go back into the game—I mean, we'd driven all this way! He said he wasn't sure, so I knew he was done for the day. I carried his helmet and stick and water bottle to the locker room, and he shambled after. A woman in a white pantsuit came in as Micah changed. She asked if we could talk. Berkshire has a nurse-practitioner on call. She apparently responds to serious on-ice incidents. What she'd seen on the close-circuit television—Micah's head hitting the ice—concerned her enough to make a visit. She asked Micah some questions, then reached into her bag. She tapped his knee with a hammer, felt his skull, looked into his eyes with a flashlight, clicking the beam on and off. If he has a concussion, she said, it's mild, but she suggested we take him to his doctor at home anyway, "just to be safe."

We were in the car before the game was over. Micah looked out the window as I drove. He said he felt "weird," like he was floating. It was the first time his soul had been separated from his body and he was enjoying it. I made him drink a lot of water and had him sit in a dark room when we got home, adding, "No video games, no screens." He was playing a game called *Clash Royale* on his computer when I checked, which infuriated me. He missed Sunday's game. On Monday, my wife took him to the doctor, who agreed that he'd probably not been concussed and said that it was OK for him to play.

I still didn't know what to do. I wanted to be safe, but I didn't want to be a ninny. I called my brother Steven. He's five years older than me, played hockey before me, peaked and declined before me, got married and became a hockey parent before me. Whatever I was living, he'd lived it before. I told him what had happened. He asked a few questions, then said, "Tell me this: Does Micah seem like himself? If he seems like himself, he's fine. Think of all the shit we went through."

When he said this, a montage of youthful injuries flashed through my memory. I saw myself flying over the handlebars of my bike, being thrown into the dashboard of a station wagon, a paramedic lifting me from the wreckage. I saw wipeouts and collisions, fights and fails that turned stars around my head. I saw myself caught looking down on the ice, getting laid out by a kid who skated away laughing. What was done in the aftermath of these concussions or near concussions? Nothing. At most, my mom would wake me in the night and ask if I remembered my name.

I sent Micah to play the next weekend, but Coach Hendrix called me over five minutes into the game. "He doesn't look right," said the coach. "I don't feel comfortable having him out there." Micah sat the rest of the week, missing three practices and two more games. Then, as I looked at the calendar, figuring out when he'd come back, my heart sank. Micah's return would be on the eve of Yom Kippur, the holiest night on the Jewish calendar, a time of atonement, when the Book of Life stands open and God decides who will live and who will die. Micah's second game back would be on Yom Kippur itself. You are supposed to be in synagogue on that day or at home fasting—not playing hockey.

I think religion is important for kids, even if they reject it. It sets the rules, establishes the ground beneath their feet. They might be lost with God, but at least they'll know they're lost. But keeping the holiday would mean Micah missing two more games. Once again, I turned to my brother, who, without hesitation, said, "Micah can't play on Yom Kippur."

"But he's already missed over a week," I whined.

"This was settled by Sandy Koufax in 1965," my brother said. "If Koufax skipped a World Series start to observe the holiday, Micah can sit out a few Pee Wee hockey games."

Micah ended up missing two weeks. When he did return, it was as if he was starting over. If I'd assumed he'd reclaim his former position—left wing on the top line, a spot he'd earned—I was wrong. He was back on the third line. Here's the thing: you stop playing, but the train rolls on. Of course I was angry. I mean, *What the fuck?* You're not supposed to lose your spot because of an injury, especially a head injury. If that were the case, no kid who wants to play would give an honest account of his symptoms. By playing on the third line, Micah would get less ice time. He'd sit out the power plays and penalty kills. All this matters: you do not play, you can't improve; you don't improve, you do not play. It's a negative feedback loop.

I tried to see it from the coach's point of view. Micah had to work his way back into game shape. He had to find his groove. What's more, other kids had performed in his absence. If Micah wanted his shift back, he'd have to take it away from them. And yet, no matter how much I tried to make the case, it still seemed wrong. It violated a philosophical tenet of every team from Mites to pros: you don't lose your position because of an injury.

I waited outside the rink for Coach Pete. I could see him, then could see him see me. He looked left, looked right, gave up, walked over, shook my hand, and said, "We're glad to have Micah back, but remember the twenty-four-hour rule." He seemed nervous about what I might say. I think he knew why I was angry and knew I was right to be angry but had Coach Hendrix to deal with, which was a bigger problem. This made me feel a little sad for Coach Pete, who, with his dark hair slicked down and face flushed, looked about fifteen years old. His father was in trouble. He didn't need me giving him a hard time. Why *did* he coach? It didn't seem like he was having fun. And he wasn't especially good at it. Maybe it made him feel important to have all these parents, who were twenty or thirty years older than him, doctors, contractors, finance guys, lining up to schmooze their kids three or four extra minutes of ice time. Maybe he did it because his brother and father had done it. Maybe he wanted to relive high school. Maybe he was bored. Maybe it was just something to do.

"It bugs me that Micah lost his spot," I said.

"I wouldn't say he lost his spot," said Coach Pete.

"Then what would you say?"

"I don't like to talk about this sort of thing, but I'm going to make an exception," Coach Pete said, leaning in. "With Micah off the ice, I noticed certain holes in our roster. The big one is that third line. Roman Holian should never have made this team. He can shoot, but he can't skate. And he can't see. We're exposed every time he's out there. Micah is one of the few kids quick enough to cover for Roman. We need his help on that third line."

I stood there, thinking. He'd complimented Micah, which is usually enough to defuse me. He must have known that. But he was also giving him a crap detail, which seemed unfair.

"Don't tell anyone what I said," Coach Pete continued. "I don't want it getting back to Roman and his parents."

"I'm still not sure it's right," I said.

"What's not right?"

"That Micah has to sacrifice his season because you guys got the tryouts wrong. Micah wanted to be on this team so he could skate with better players."

"Let me ask you this," said Coach Pete, trying a different strategy. "Is Micah happy?"

"Yes."

"Is Micah having fun?"

"Yes."

"So what do you care? Try to remember what this is about—them, not us. It's about learning the sport but also learning to be part of a team. Sometimes you have to do something you don't want to do for the good of the team, like in a family."

This made me think of Coach Pete's father. I did not want

to add to the coach's troubles, so I nodded and went into the rink to wait for Micah. Though I chatted amicably with other parents, I was troubled. On the one hand, I got it. On the other hand, I wanted to know why—assuming that Coach Pete was telling the truth—my kid had to take the bullet. Why not ask one of the parent-coaches' kids to cover for Roman? It made me think of the movie *North Dallas Forty*, in which an NFL receiver confronts his coach, who is asking him to sacrifice for the team. Pointing to the club owner, the player says, "Don't you get it? We're not the team. These guys right here, they're the team. We're the equipment."

I expected Micah to be angry about being moved back to the third line, but he talked only about Mike and Ikes as we drove home. (He wants candy after a game the way a pirate wants rum.) He did not even seem to know that he'd been shafted. He just seemed happy to be back. I was irritated by this lack of concern. I'd been steeling myself to console him, to explain the nature of life, but he didn't care.

"What's wrong with you?" I asked.

"What do you mean?"

"Did you notice that you're off the first line?"

His eyes fell, the air went out of him.

"Yes," he said softly.

"Doesn't it bother you?" I asked. "Why aren't you pissed off?"

It was a recurring gripe of mine: Micah never seemed to get angry. I was the opposite when I played. I was mad the entire time. It's what motivated me, anger and a desire for revenge. I was always being screwed, undervalued, put on the wrong line, disrespected, treated like trash. It gave me an edge. I loved hockey, but did not enjoy it. I was too angry. My only goal was to prove that my coaches, teammates, opponents, parents, and siblings had been wrong.

Micah plays happy. He loves being part of a team—wearing the jacket, walking with a gaggle of teammates through town. He smiles when he skates, which is weird. Maybe it's because they took checking out of the pre-Bantam game. He lives in a world without predators. Or maybe he just has a sunny disposition. I've tried to impart my sense of urgency. Before a big game, I once said, "The kids on the other team are not just trying to win. They're trying to humiliate you. That's how you should look at it." But it didn't take. Whereas I played hot, he played cool. I eventually came to see this as a gift. It's not his skating, nor puck control, nor hockey sense that makes him a good player. It's his joy.

"Does it bother you at all?" I finally asked.

"Not much," he admitted.

"Why not?"

"Because, no matter where they put me, it's still hockey."

Our next game was at the Darien Ice House. Every car in the parking lot told you that these people were richer, more fulfilled, and flat-out better than us.

Ridgefield occupies the cozy middle on the local socioeconomic scale—not a great spot for athletes. Blue-collar towns like Winchester and Bridgeport beat us because their kids are tougher. Wealthy towns like New Canaan and Greenwich beat us because they pay for better instructors. Most of our coaches never played past high school. For a time, the Connecticut Junior Rangers Pee Wee team in Greenwich were coached by NHL Hall of Famer Martin St. Louis. (One parent, having not been briefed on St. Louis's career, cursed him, saying, "You don't know the first thing about this game!") The Bears were playing the North Darien Lady Wings, an elite all-girls team. They were more skilled than us, as clearly stated in Coach Hendrix's scouting report. (He'd seen them twice in person, once on LiveBarn.) In my day, you'd have neutralized their speed with violence. Stand 'em up at the blue line, pancake 'em in the corner. But checking is verboten. Besides, we'd all raised our boys with the same admonition: "Never hit a girl."

I knew we were in trouble before the game started. In most cases, when a team has finished getting dressed, the players stand along the Plexiglas, watching the Zamboni. No one is allowed on the ice till the machine is parked and the refs have skated out. The Lady Wings had choreographed a more dramatic entrance. As our players were going through their warm-ups, "Crazy Train" blared from a loudspeaker, the locker room door flew open, and out came the Lady Wings, one at a time, as if shot from a canon. They sprinted to the rink door, hopped onto the ice, skated a fast lap, then cohered into an intricate Blue Angels–like figure eight, fifteen girls in pink jerseys whirling into a void. Our players stopped and stared. Jerry Sherman yelled from the bleachers, "Don't look! They're sirens!"

Coach Pete had scrambled the lines. Tommy McDermott would center the first with Broadway Jenny Hendrix at right wing and Leo Moriarty at left. Coach Pete told the centers to play aggressive. "I don't care if they're girls," he said, "use your body. Get the puck!"

Tommy stood eye-to-eye with the Lady Wings' top skater,

a girl named Gallagher. A blond ponytail hung from the back of her helmet. He hesitated when the puck was dropped. She swung her shoulder into his chest, knocking him back. Gallagher played the puck back to a defenseman, who, in one smooth motion, gathered and skated it around Patrick Campi, then sent a long pass up ice to the right wing. What happened next is called "tic-tac-toe." The Lady Wings zipped the puck back and forth, back and forth, back and forth, until our defense was mesmerized. Gallagher finished the play by putting the puck through Dan Arcus's legs—called the "five-hole." The horn blew, the North Darien parents cheered. And just like that, we felt like patsies, less like the parents of hockey players and more like the parents of props. *Bing. Bang. Boom.* It had happened so fast. Our section of the bleachers was quiet. The silence was broken by a single voice. It was Parky Taylor saying, "Jesus H. Christ."

There's a debate in the world of youth hockey: What should a coach do after his team has been scored on? Traditionalists tell you to change lines immediately, even if the kids have only been on for ten seconds. You don't reward failure with more ice time. Statisticians do not only record goals and assists, after all, but also how many goals a team scores when a certain player is on the ice versus how many goals are scored against the team when that player is on. The sum of these numbers is called the plus-minus. It's probably the most important statistic in the game. Plus 5 is good. Minus 8 is bad. Pull the line that picked up the minus, let them sit and think about why they failed—that's the old way. To a hockey progressive, this seems counterproductive, mean. If the line has been out less than a minute—the Lady Wings scored fifteen seconds into the first period—let them finish their shift. Who will be more motivated to get back that goal than the kids who let it in?

Coach Pete was a hockey progressive, which made him suspect to some of the parents. You could hear muttering when he sent the first line back for another face-off. Judd Meese, our oldest parent, sighed and said, "That's what's wrong with America."

Tommy lost the next face-off, too. The Lady Wings headed up ice once again. Broadway Jenny tried to block Gallagher, who blew right past. It came down to a one-on-one, Gallagher versus defenseman Brian Rizzo, who stepped up for a steal but missed the puck, taking himself out of the play. Gallagher scored—faked low, beat Arcus high. He slammed his stick against the crossbar, pushed back his mask, and took a drink of water. Patrick went over to talk to him. Arcus listened with his head down. Something Patrick said made him laugh. He looked better after that. And yet, the Lady Wings continued to score. Once on our second line, twice on our third, once more on our first.

Becky Goodman was solid on defense, but the rest of them were, to quote Jerry Sherman, "playing like they did bong hits in the locker room." They became confused, turned the wrong way, gave up when beaten. Rizzo had a habit of passing the puck in front of our own goal—you knew when it happened because you could hear Jocko Arcus bang on the glass and moan. Late in the second period, Rizzo and Stanley crashed into each other and both fell down, leaving the puck in the middle of the ice. "You should be seeing the front of a defenseman," Parky Taylor told me. "You know. The eyes and chest and knees as the kid skates backward. All I'm seeing today is Rizzo's back."

One of their goals came when we were shorthanded, having taken a dumb penalty. Duffy, acting in frustration, checked a Lady Wing from behind. Some of the Darien parents hissed. Coach Pete lectured Duffy as he sat in the penalty box, sweating and suffering. Coach Pete kept Duffy on the bench for most of the game after that. I hoped this meant Micah could move to the second line and skate with some of the playmakers, but Broadway Jenny, the coach's kid, double-shifted instead. We were down 5–0 late in the second. Hockey is not Little League. There is no slaughter rule. The algorithm wants massacres. You either regroup or take a beating.

The entire team went onto the ice between periods. They stood in a half circle around Coach Pete, who spoke from the bench. He was not big on inspiration. He did not make speeches. He was buttoned-up, technical, nuts-and-bolts. He held up a wipe board and drew lines to show what he wanted each player to do. His strategy looked complicated from a distance, as if he were describing his honeymoon itinerary. When I asked Micah what Coach Pete talked about, he said, "He told us to keep shooting. He said that if we took fifty shots, at least seven were bound to go in."

The Bears had more jump in the third period. They finally seemed to know what they wanted to do: crowd the Lady Wings, clog the passing lanes, gum up the works, test the goalie. The score was 6–2 in the middle of the period when the Lady Wings seemed to run out of gas. Their skating slowed, as did their passes; their shots drifted like struck birds. We scored, then scored again. A wrist shot Barry took from the left hash mark—the parallel lines on either side of the face-off circles at each end of the rink—hit the inside of the Darien net so hard it made the goalie's water bottle jump.

We were down by a goal with three minutes left in the game. From that point on, the Bears skated just the two top lines. Micah, Broadway Julie, and Roman were done for the day, turned into spectators, no different from the parents in the stands. It put me in a strange spot. I cheered for the team but secretly wanted them to fail. If this worked, I was afraid Micah would never see the last two minutes of a game again.

Coach Pete pulled the goalie with fifty-eight seconds left, which meant he could put on an extra skater. I was hoping for Micah, but it turned out to be Duffy, skating for the first time since his penalty. With fifteen seconds left to play, Gallagher took a wild shot from center ice. The puck went up on its side and rolled into our net.

The rest of the Lady Wings came over the boards when the buzzer sounded and piled on their goalie. The girls grinned through the handshakes. Micah was in back of the line, head down, mumbling as he grasped each outstretched palm: "Good game, good game, good game . . ." Our kids looked like mourners as they emerged from the locker room. I sent Micah to the car, then grabbed Coach Pete, promising myself, "This is the last time I will break the twenty-four-hour rule."

"I'm OK with what you said yesterday," I told Coach Pete, "but Micah not getting any ice for the last five minutes just seems wrong, for him and for all the kids on the third line."

Coach Pete looked at me, confused. "Really? Micah didn't play in the last five minutes?"

"No."

"I didn't notice," he said. "Coach Hendrix works the door. Half the time I don't even know who's out there."

But when I asked Coach Hendrix, he said, "Don't ask me. All I do is open and close the door."

Sunday night. I-95 North. America's bleakest highway. We drive in silence. Malaise drifts off the sixteen-wheelers. Even Micah feels it. I'm thinking about the game and all the work I have to do before another weekend comes around. He's thinking about school. It's dark at 5:00 p.m.

"Let's get dinner," I say, exiting near Stamford.

The stores are closed, the houses dark. We drive through a small town. There's a village hall and a public square with a statue of a WWI doughboy. It's nights like this that made Eugene O'Neill long for Communist Russia. I park in front of a diner. The windows are aglow. It's a refuge on a desolate shore, a clean, well-lighted place. We go in and order cheese-burgers. As we look for a table, I spot Parky and Duffy in a corner. Having finished his meal, Parky is eyeing Duffy's food. He looks up when I say hello, smiles sadly, and says, "I can't stand this season."

"Don't give up," I tell him. "There's still a lot more hockey to play."

Thus began a listless run of practices and games—a losing streak, a funk—that those who believe in curses would call star-crossed. Get out *Fodor's New England* and check the index for Connecticut. We lost in every one of those towns. We lost in Greenwich, Southport, Fairfield, Norwalk, Bridgeport. We lost in Kent, Washington, and Westport. We lost in both Milfords and several Havens. Some games were close; in others, we were blown out. "There's nothing to learn from a game like that," Coach Pete said after a shellacking in Simsbury. "Just go home and forget it." Some teams were better than we were. Others hustled more. Some had a better goalie. Others had a better coach. Some got lucky. Some had a better plan. Some were gracious in victory. Others were cruel. Some talked trash. Others talked trash *and* played dirty. The Pee Wee A Bears imbibed an adult portion of shame in those weeks. It was an echoing spiral. The more they lost, the worse they felt. The worse they felt, the worse they played and the more they lost. Down we went, until the biggest question, the only real mystery, was, How deep does this hole go?

Meanwhile, the story behind the story—the probable source of the funk—had been unfolding in a Hartford courthouse, where Coach Pete's father, convicted of wire fraud, theft, and embezzlement, awaited sentencing. Coach Pete must have been anxiously anticipating, on hold till he knew the shape of his family's future. None of the other parents seemed to be clued in, or maybe they were being discreet. I could not stop imagining the sorry affair, the middle-aged man and the young woman for whom he'd sacrificed everything. How did Coach Pete keep smiling and drawing plays through it all? He was either numb inside, or very tough and brave. At practices and games he behaved as if nothing else were happening. Maybe hockey was his escape, the place he kept his old identity, which is one reason I did not ask about his father. If this was his bubble, I would not pop it.

Losing affected the mood on the bench, the behavior of

the kids, everything. They bickered, became unruly. Patrick threw a puck. It hit Duffy, who, or so Micah said, spit out a tooth, smiled and called Patrick an F-tard, though now with a lisp. Rick brought a pizza to the locker room, which was verboten, then made things worse by sharing it with only select teammates—Roman, Leo, Joey. Brian took a piece anyway. Rick threw the box aside, stood, and said, "You wanna go? Let's go!" Blows were exchanged. After a loss in New Canaan, Brian's mother sent Brian's sister into the locker room to tell Brian to hurry up. Tommy made a gross sexual remark. Brian punched Tommy, sparking a general melee. Standing in his underwear and prescription goggles, Roman shouted, "Who wants to fuck me? I'll fuck anyone who wants to fuck me." Coach Rizzo tried to have Tommy suspended. When the board dismissed this suggestion as unnecessarily harsh, he asked that Tommy be made to dress alone. This too was rejected.

"Where I come from," said Jocko Arcus. "You're either on the team or off the team."

"Not to mention the fact that, without Tommy, we'd never win another game," Jerry Sherman added.

But here's the thing about hockey: it's good even when it's bad. There's always the possibility of a breakaway, life on the rush, how the puck feels on your stick. And of course there's the culture of the game, the values, philosophy, minutiae. There are the rinks, the ice palaces and winter gardens, each different but all the same, the smell of sweat and hum of industrial equipment, exhaust fans, pumping units, and chillers. There are the lobbies with soda, candy, and claw machines and of course the vintage pinball and arcade games—*PAC-MAN, Defender, Galaxian.* There's the Zamboni driver finishing his task with broom and scraper, smoothing the lip of ice that accumulates in front of the big doors where the Zamboni sleeps. There are rink rats with tape balls, chewing tobacco, tall tales, and broken sticks mined from the dumpster. There are TVs showing great games from hockey's past. There is satellite radio to fill all the hours on the road. Micah and I would listen to New York Rangers games on the way and to Los Angeles Kings games on the way back. We agreed that a game can be even better on the radio. "With television, the game is played on a screen," Micah explained. "On radio, it's played in your head." He liked when the announcers were quiet and you could hear the crowd, the hoots and whistles, the slap of the puck. We'd argue about players. He championed the stars of the moment: Connor McDavid, Sidney Crosby, Patrick Kane. Being an old man, I liked the old-timers: Wayne Gretzky, Mark Messier, Stan Mikita.

I told Micah the history of the sport, how it likely started on frozen ponds in western Canada and then moved indoors. I told him how it evolved, what it had been, and why it changed. I told him about the famous arenas: the Montreal Forum, the Boston Garden, and the old Madison Square Garden, where the Brooklyn Americans played on the same ice as the Rangers. I told him about the renowned NHL teams, the villains and heroes. I told him about the 1977 Canadiens, and the 1982 Islanders, and the 1984 Oilers, and the 2013 Blackhawks. I told him about the first goalie to wear a face mask, the first player to curve a stick. I was introducing him not just to a history, but to an ethos and lore. I wanted him to become a citizen of Hockey Nation. I wanted to give him something he could enjoy long after he stopped playing.

"Every team loses the way your team is losing now," I told him. "It's important. It can even be seen as a kind of opportunity. You don't learn by winning: you learn by losing. You have to go through it. That's how you become a hockey player. We all get knocked down. Who gets back up? That's the question."

I showed him the hockey cards I'd collected in the 1970s. Each pack came with a booklet, a cartoon biography of a player who grew up in the 1940s or 1950s. These were fables, morality plays. They all started the same way: with a kid too poor to buy equipment fashioning a puck out of an old pair of socks, pads out of an old mattress. He'd turn up in hand-me-down skates at the pond only to be laughed at and driven away. He practiced alone. He was the young David sent to tend sheep while his brothers battled the Philistines. When Goliath appears in the valley, he will emerge. The comics all ended the same way, too: with a young player, Denis Potvin or Greg Polis or Brad Park, sticks in hand, bag on shoulder, staring at the facade of Chicago Stadium or Maple Leaf Gardens—the promised land!

We watched hockey movies. *Miracle*, in which Kurt Russell plays Herb Brooks, coach of the 1980 U.S. Olympic team that shocked the Soviets in Lake Placid, New York. "You think you can win on talent alone?" Brooks tells his players. "Gentlemen, you don't have enough talent to win on talent alone." *Youngblood*, in which Rob Lowe plays a prospect making the transition from amateur hockey to the game's violent minor leagues. The Blackhawks' brawler Eric Nesterenko, playing Lowe's father, teaches Lowe to fight. "You can learn to punch in the barn," Nesterenko says, "but you gotta learn to survive on the ice." And of course we repeat-watched *Slap Shot*, in which Paul Newman plays Reggie Dunlop, aging player-coach of the Charlestown Chiefs of the Federal League.

"Let 'em know you're out there," Reg tells his team. "Get that fucking stick in their side! Let 'em know you're there! Get that lumber in his teeth! Let 'em know you're there!"

As you make your way through this oeuvre, one question keeps recurring: What's the best way to turn a kid into an athlete or any kind of artist?

There are two basic approaches: force or enticement. You can think of it in terms of broad pedagogical concepts, or you can imagine two fathers, each with his own parenting style.

First, there's Press Maravich, the father of basketball prodigy Pete Maravich. Press, who played pro basketball for the Youngstown Bears and the Pittsburgh Ironmen, had made the transition to coaching by the time Pete was born in Aliquippa, Pennsylvania, in 1947. Pete began to show interest in basketball as soon as he could walk, yet, disturbingly for Press, he showed interest in football and music, too. Press responded with reverse psychology: he'd host pickup basketball games at his house but refuse to let Pete so much as touch the ball. Pete sat in the window watching. He came to know the basics even before he could dribble. Press finally "gave in" and let Pete play. *OK. I can't stop you.* Pete—later known as "Pistol" because he shot from the hip, like a gunfighter—had been hooked by forbidden fruit. The way he moved, how he carried the ball, the don't-look passes, and the shots that came off the rebound—his game had the joy of something sinful. He scored fifty points in his college debut. He averaged 44.2 points a game at Louisiana State University, where he was coached by his father. He became a national sensation. His floppy hair, saggy socks, and lope were imitated by kids across the country. He was taken third in the 1970 NBA draft. He was a great player on a mediocre team in Atlanta, what the franchise gave its fans instead of victory. He served the same function when he played in New Orleans. He was not on a good pro team until 1980, when he was signed by the Boston Celtics partly to mentor the rookie Larry Bird. Pete's knees were shot by then; the picture of him packed in ice at the end of the bench is pure American melancholy, what the game does to beautiful youth. He retired at thirty-two and died eight years later, collapsing during a pickup basketball game. An autopsy showed he'd been born missing a coronary artery on the left side. He shouldn't have been able to run, let alone play the way he played for over twenty years. His was a miracle, driven by the desire of a kid forbidden to play. He was convinced that he'd chosen his course, though it had been chosen for him. That's the Press Maravich method.

There was no illusion of freedom for Andre Agassi, whose father, Mike, plotted his course in the way of a mountain climber. Mike, an Iranian immigrant who started in this country as a doorman in Chicago, recognized tennis as a back way into the upper class, and so had his son on a court before he was strong enough to hold a racquet. He made Andre hit five thousand tennis balls every morning, afternoon, and night. If there was a conflict with school, there was no school. Andre came to hate tennis but stayed with it because Mike would not let him quit. Mike Agassi was Malcolm Gladwell's dream father, working his son like a thoroughbred—no freedom, no joy, just the long road to ten thousand hours. Tennis stopped being a game for Andre before he was ten years old. It was early mornings, screaming adults, impossible standards, the end of childhood. It's the Mike Agassi method that made Andre Agassi into one of the greatest tennis players in the world.

Which brings us to another question, the only one that really matters: What do you want out of the game?

For most parents and kids it's about fun as well as the lessons that come from the experience, lessons that can be applied to the rest of life. *Teamwork means sacrifice; effort means playing through pain.* A good player learns to plan for the future. You don't pass to a teammate. You pass to the place that teammate will be in the future. You learn the art of friendship. The violence of the sport increases intimacy. You become comrades facing a threat. Feelings of appreciation and equality emerge: I don't care what you look like, only if you can help get us out of this jam. But losing is the game's great teacher, even if you'd rather not sit through the lessons. Even a good season will include slumps and spirals, moments of fury and walks of shame. The game is ecclesiastical. It teaches the folly of pride. "Vanity of vanities; all is vanity." It lectures on human limitations. No matter how good you are, someone is better. Losing is humbling. "In much wisdom is much grief; and he that increaseth knowledge increaseth sorrow." You shouldn't like losing, but must know how to do it. Being a good loser means not blaming the refs, even if the refs were at fault. It means knowing when the game is over. It means crediting the other team. The handshake line that follows even the most contentious game is hockey's greatest ritual. It's a way of saying, "That is finished and we accept each other and continue on with our lives." Being a good loser means learning these lessons, then leaving the loss behind. If you brood, you will lose again. That's how a bad game turns into a slump.

Winning has its lessons, too. We all hate sore losers, but sore winners are worse. Be modest in victory, knowing you could just as easily have been on the other side, as you were yesterday and will be tomorrow. Don't be a wise guy. Don't chirp. Don't say "ha-ha" in the handshake line. Follow the golden rule. In my day, we raised our sticks when we scored to draw attention. The modern kid goes in for more elaborate celebrations, fist-pumping, pointing. And yet, even in the NHL, hockey celebrations come nowhere near the decadence of the touchdown dance. Our game is the best kind of throwback: a fortress against a pagan tide of gloating. A few years ago, when a New York Ranger, having scored, pretended his stick was a rifle, then, looking through the scope, pretended to assassinate the goalie, he was denounced even by his own teammates.

NOVEMBER

A bitter wind drove the last of the leaves from the trees. The roads were icy in the morning. The hills dreamt of snow. Hemingway said bare trees are OK once you accept them as modern sculpture, but it's a trick I could never manage. The season that comes after the leaves and before the snow makes me want to cry. Some say it's the lack of light, the earth spinning away from the sun. In November, the only dependable light is rink light. We live as if in a terrarium.

The Bears had been losing for what felt like eternity. After the ninth consecutive defeat, the kids had learned all they could from the experience. It was just pain from there, as coaches turned on players, and players turned on each other, and parents pontificated and proposed, "What if we skate five forwards?" In the end, you stop scheming and instead wait for the clap of thunder that signals the end of drought. It came in the middle of November in a town in the center of Connecticut. I was not sure where I was, but I knew it was in the middle—the middle of the state, the middle of the season, and the middle of my life.

The town itself was nothing but boarded windows and shuttered stores. "It looks like this place never got over the recession of '08," said Parky Taylor, sipping from his supersize coffee.

"More like the crash of '29," said Jerry Sherman.

The rink was in a sheet-metal warehouse that creaked in the wind. It felt haunted. You glimpsed the ghosts of hockey past, players in Lange skates with plastic boots, Super Tacks, Stan Mikita helmets, and the sort of exterior mouthguards that dominated in the '70s, a time of great bloodletting. The locker room was small, low-ceilinged, and hot as a schvitz. There were no benches and no cubbies in the visitors' clubhouse. The hooks had been removed from the walls. The Bears had to sit on the floor to lace their skates. This is called gamesmanship, home advantage. Even the ice was strange, damp and small, surrounded by rickety boards that yielded crazy bounces. We must have passed through a portal on I-84—this was like a visit to an earlier place in hockey time.

The Ridgefield parents sat on one side of the bleachers, the home team parents on the other. The kids came out through a tunnel between. The home team parents jeered at our kids. The Ridgefield parents jeered back. The arena was soon in an uproar. There are just a few rules for spectators at a youth hockey game, and the hometowners had broken three of them before the first puck dropped: they heckled; they swore; they blasted an air horn, the sort that clears your sinuses.

"Oh Lord, look!" said Jerry Sherman, pointing at the home team goalie, who was leading his players onto the ice.

Once upon a time, kids wanted to play goalie for a single reason: the face masks, which, in the 1970s, were still the kind worn by the psycho in *Friday the 13th*. Imaginative goalies painted their masks, a burst of creativity in an otherwise conformist culture. Certain NHL netminders became known less for prowess than for artistry: Gary Bromley, whose nickname was Bones—the guy was skinny as a rail—painted his mask to look like a skull, which was called Skeletor; Gilles Gratton of the New York Rangers painted his to look like a tiger; Gerry Cheevers of the Boston Bruins painted stitches everywhere a puck had hit his mask, showing what his face would've looked like had he played in the iron age. By the 1980s, fiberglass masks had given way to cages, which offer better protection. Yet here was the hometown goalie in an old-fashioned nonregulation mask painted to look like a grinning red devil.

Coach Pete sent Barry Meese out for the opening face-off—at this point, the coaches were juggling the lines, looking for a spark. Barry played the puck to Leo, who quickly found himself in a battle along the boards, which ended with Leo *and* Barry on their backs as the hometown center skated away, setting the tone for what followed. As a group, the other team was slow, dogged, and rough. They held our skaters by the jerseys, stood in front of their shots, and whacked their legs. They seemed to be following a flood-the-zone-to-overwhelm strategy: if they all committed penalties simultaneously all over the ice, the refs would catch only a fraction. Their forwards came out for warm-ups each carrying four or five sticks—wooden cheapies, the sort that sell for ten bucks in the pro shop's used bin—which should have told us they'd been planning to lay the lumber.

Micah was centering the third line but could do nothing with the puck. If it did not hop over his stick, he lost it to whatever kid was hanging on his back. Brian, Joey, Broadway Julie, Rick, Tommy, and Jack Camus were all being stymied in the same way. Dan was doing his best in goal, but a few shots found their way into our net. It was 3–0 at the start of the second period. The home team parents had been taunting so much that we actually stopped noticing. Our kids were not only losing; they were getting bullied. It was hard to watch. At such times you wonder why you filled the car with gas and drove all this way. When one of our forwards did get past their defense—I'm thinking of Joey, who made a deft pivot— he found himself staring into the grinning eyes of that red devil in the net.

Coach Pete called a time-out. Our kids stood around, shoulders slumped, listless. Their body language sucked. They looked as if they could not wait for the game and even the season to be over. Nothing is sadder than a sad kid on skates. Duffy was the only Bear who had not given up. The refs had stopped calling any but the most blatant penalties, making it his kind of game. He said something to Coach Pete, who let him take the face-off after the time-out. He won it, kept the puck, headed up ice, lost the puck, got it back, passed, re- ceived a pass, lost it again. He was all over the place. His feet never stopped moving. Somebody hacked him, he hacked back. Somebody shoved him, he shoved back. You could see that he was getting angrier and angrier. He could not ignore the slightest discourtesy. You could hear the ticking. You knew at some point he would explode. It was Coach Pete's job to channel Duffy's rage. Hotheaded kids often turn out to be the kids with the most potential; they hate to lose and can't stand to be shown up. But our coaches failed Duffy and, hav- ing failed, gave up on him. Which only made him angrier, thus more likely to erupt.

The home team had a player named Eli Malachi. I know

this because while most kids have just their last name on their jersey, Eli Malachi had the whole thing: *Eli Malachi*. He was a good player, but arrogant and heedless in his arrogance. He skated with his head down. Half the time, he did not know where he was. Late in the second, he carried the puck blindly through the neutral zone, the middle of the ice between the two blue lines. You could not see his face, but knew it was clever and mean. He looked up as Duffy moved in and, in looking up, lost the puck in his skates. Duffy reached for the puck and skated right through Eli Malachi. He was sent sprawling. The ref blew the whistle. A blast of air horn, a ring of cowbell. A parent's voice could be heard above the din: "That little bastard almost killed Eli Malachi!" When Eli Malachi sat up, you could see birds twittering around his head. He did not know where he was. Then he did. He got to his feet, crying and shouting.

Duffy served two minutes in the penalty box for roughing. The hometown parents were infuriated. They wanted Duffy tossed, but he was back before the end of the period, skating like a dynamo, fast and with purpose, poke-checking, lifting sticks, driving the net. He got off a hard shot as the buzzer sounded. It rang off the post, the most frustrating sound in hockey. As the players skated back to their benches, Eli Malachi hopped over the boards and went for Duffy. He turned his stick around and carried it like a lance. He speared Duffy below the ribs, a place unprotected by pads. Duffy fell to his knees. Players came together, shoving. The coaches and refs broke it up. Duffy was helped off the ice, one arm around Coach Hendrix, the other around Coach Rizzo. Eli Malachi had his helmet off and was being lectured by the official. We could hear him explaining himself: "Nobody touches Eli Malachi! Nobody!"

Between periods, our players gathered around Coach Pete.

"Make one play," he implored. "That's all we need: one play."

He wrote it on the wipe board and held the words before the kids: "ONE PLAY!"

The Bears were distracted by the home team coach, who was screaming at his players: "This is not the time to relax," he shouted. "This is the time to bury these losers. You know what they are? Turds! We've got turds in the toilet! And what do we do with turds? We flush 'em! Now get out there and flush these turds!"

"I agree with the second part," said Jerry Sherman.

"What's that?" asked Parky.

"That that's what you do with turds," said Jerry. "It's the first part, the part about our kids *being* turds, that I dispute."

I could hear Simone Camus muttering, "*Mon Dieu, mon Dieu.*"

Micah took the face-off to start the third. He was playing

with Broadway Julie on right wing and Roman Holian on left. He sent the puck back to Brian Rizzo, who was playing defense on the right side. Brian passed cross-ice to his defensive partner, Joey McDermott, who took off. Joey is so small that you forget his speed. He blew by the opposing wings, then blew by the defense. He passed to Micah, who passed to Broadway Julie, who was waiting just outside the crease. She held the puck long enough for the devil in net to slide over, then passed—a saucer pass, it hopped a defender's stick—to Roman, who was beside the left goalpost. He finished with a snap shot.

GOAL!

The players on the Bears bench went wild, hooting, banging their sticks on the boards. Jerry Sherman pounded me and Parky on the back. Parky choked on a pretzel. I spilled my coffee. In that moment, the team, which had touched bottom, began to surface. Coach Pete was correct. One play—that's all it took. Even better that it was the sort of play that involves every Bear on the ice. Sometimes you root less for the team than for the game itself, for seeing a thing done well.

Everything clicked from there. Tommy scored on the next shift, a breakaway. Barry scored after that. He scored from behind the net, bouncing the puck off the goalie's leg, which is like punching a kid with his own fist. Broadway Jenny popped in a rebound late in the third, giving the Bears their first lead in weeks.

The score was 5–4 with twenty seconds left. The top line went out to finish it. Barry won the face-off, passed to Brian, who passed to Joey, who skated with the puck till the horn blew. The Bears swarmed Dan. I could hear them chanting, "Arc, Arc, Arc, Arc."

Jerry Sherman texted me that night:

> JS: A triumph, huh? I'm still flying. Just glad we got
> out in one piece. I spotted gun stickers on every
> windshield in the parking lot. All pickup trucks.
> RC: I saw a backhoe.
> JS: To bury the dead!
> RC: Well, we're alive. And we won. Finally.
> RC: What do you think did it?
> JS: Turd speech. No one likes being called a turd.

And so began a time of success, the salad days. A winning streak is a losing streak in negative. Whereas the Pee Wee A Bears once felt they could neither defend nor score, they came to believe they could not be stopped. This made them happy. They lingered in that happiness, taking more and more time in the locker room, blasting "Welcome to the Jungle," "Dude Looks Like a Lady," "Hot for Teacher," emerging wet-haired, smiling. Tommy showed up with a pack of condoms, which he inflated and floated and punched. The kids loved one another again, hung out after games, had sleepovers, walked through town in their jackets like a victorious army. Micah bought a box of snappers at the toy store, which, whenever he heard something he liked, he'd throw at the ground. These were confiscated by Coach Hendrix. The more they loved each other, the better they played. The better they played, the more they loved each other. What had been a negative feed-back loop gave way to a virtuous cycle.

It was a group effort of course, but if you wanted to credit a single player, it'd be our goalie Dan Arcus. Tall, olive-skinned with warm brown eyes, shy and distracted off the ice but practiced in the art of high focus between the pipes, he was brilliant throughout the streak, a highlight reel, a catalog of every kind of save: the butterfly, the split, blocker and glove. Goalie is the toughest position in hockey. Within the ecosystem of the ultimate team sport, the goalie remains an individual, solitary and intense. He succeeds and fails, lives and dies, alone. It takes a certain type. When the puck is on the far side of the ice, two hundred feet away, he has nothing to do but wait. What does he think about? What does he see? When fortunes shift and the opponent heads the opposite way on the rush, two or three forwards passing the puck or a hotshot coming in alone, the goalie shifts from the periphery to the center of the action. Imagine it: eight kids coming at you full stride, your defensemen, just their backs, gliding in like recalled kites, everyone on the move but you, the object of it all, pinned between the posts, trapped in the prisonlike crease. When the team wins, the goalie is hardly credited. Most of the glory goes to the scorers. When the team loses, the goalie takes most of the blame. "If only Dan had not given up that soft goal," Coach Hendrix says, shaking his head. The goalie is different from the others, set off by the uniqueness of his task and the oddity of his equipment. Even his skates are different. His blades are flat instead of curved, to give him stability and lateral movement. His only compatriot is the backup goalie—we didn't even have one—who is also his only rival. It'd be enough to make anyone crazy, hence the famous eccentricity of the netminder.

Question: Does the job make the goalie nuts, or do only nutty people apply?

Goalies have been known to touch every corner of the net before a face-off. Some twitch when not engaged. All drink water immediately after getting scored on, even if not thirsty, leaning on the crossbar as if they're having a beer at the pub—they do this to tell the world and themselves that they remain calm and unperturbed. The Blackhawks' goalie Glenn Hall used to vomit in the locker room before games. Nerves. The Canadiens' goalie Patrick Roy developed a kind of ice-only Tourette's. He'd curse and tic all game, and talk to the goal posts, who were always dressed in red. Though just twelve years old, Arcus had already developed weird habits. He'd eat only McNuggets with barbecue sauce on game days. If given sweet and sour, he'd blow. He tapped his forehead against the crossbar before each face-off. He sang the Ludacris song "Get Back" between periods:

> *See I caught 'em wit a right hook, caught 'em wit a jab*
> *Caught 'em wit an uppercut, kicked 'em in his ass . . .*
> *Get back motherfucker! You don't know me like that!*

We questioned none of it, not even the profanity, because it was working. In those weeks, we won in Hamden, Norwalk, Brewster, and Greenwich, defeating teams named Cougars, Panthers, Ducks, and Turtles. We won close games and blowouts. Whenever possible, we ran up the score—this was our tribute to the algorithm. We went online to check our ranking. We started November ranked fifty-second in the state. By the end of the month, we were forty-seventh. As our ultimate goal was to catch the Double As, we checked their rank, too. Having begun the season at fifth, they'd fallen to thirty-third by November. It was the talk of the organization. The Double A team, which was supposed to be the jewel of the program, had won just five games.

What was happening?

Everyone had an opinion. Many blamed the tryouts. They spoke of a "scouting-combine effect," referencing the annual NFL camp ("The Combine") where pro football coaches put college prospects through drills and tests, scoring and assessing them ahead of the draft. Since the combine started in the 1980s, NFL teams have come to overvalue the things that can be measured (height, strength, speed) and undervalue the sort of intangibles (intelligence, creativity, will) that make for winning teams. As a result, many teams are stocked with great athletes who can't really play. Had something similar happened here? The Double As had all the top skaters, but it seemed we had more intuitive hockey players.

Gordon Campi thought it was about corruption. "If you figure out why the Double As are no good," he said, "you'll understand what's wrong with the way talent is judged in this country. It's like college admissions," he explained. "They say there are fifteen roster spots, but half of them are filled before the first tryout. They go to the children of the parent-coaches and their pals, or to the sons and daughters of board members. No more than six or seven spots are genuinely in play.

The Double A coach—Jamie McRae, whom everyone called Mack—tried to fix his team midseason, on the fly. The easiest way was by replacing the goalie. A strong netminder can carry a weak team. The Double As did not have a strong netminder. They had a big, slow, easily distracted kid whose mom was on the board and whose dad worked in Zamboni maintenance—he serviced the rink's 552AC. Good goaltending is the art of deep concentration. A good goalie can fix on a puck and follow its every flip and spin for an hour. A great goalie attains a level of presence sought by yogis. A great goalie lives in the now. The Double A goalie dwelled on his mistakes, which is living in the past. If he had a good game, it was a shutout. As soon as he'd given up one goal, he'd give up three. If he gave up three, he'd give up seven.

Coach Mack, scruffy and irritable, with a dirty blond beard, began showing up at our practices. He'd sit by himself in the bleachers, never taking his eyes off Arcus. One night, after everyone else had left, I saw him talking with Dan and his parents, Jocko and Camille, on the home bench. The rink was closing; the lights had been set to dim. There were rumors that night. The next day, several of our parents cornered Jocko and Camille in the parking lot. We stood around their Dodge Charger asking questions. We wanted to know if Dan had been offered a spot on the Double A team, and if so, would he take it? The Arcuses seemed upset by the whole thing. "It's a shitty position for a kid," Jocko said. "If Dan should be a Double A, he should've been on that team from the start. What were the tryouts for anyway?"

"We have our opinions, but we're going to let Danny decide," Camille told us.

"It's his life," said Jocko.

Dan was in the Single A locker room before the next practice.

I saw Jocko and Camille in the lobby.

"Does this mean Dan's staying?" I asked.

"Yup," said Jocko. "The kid did good."

"You have to be loyal to your team," Camille added, smiling.

All this was supposed to be kept from the kids, but of course it got out. It's a good thing too, as the team bonded in a new way. Everyone worked harder after that. They wanted to prove Dan had made the right choice.

Coach Hendrix spent his non-hockey life traveling back and forth from Purchase, where he drove a golf cart around the PepsiCo perimeter. He'd once been an officer in the army, but those days were long gone. Like the rest of us, he'd thickened as he aged. He was a stout, gray-haired man in his fifties who was always chewing on something—a toothpick, a pencil, a piece of gum. He never seemed less than a little angry. His older daughter had played hockey but quit. It was easy to understand why. Coach Hendrix tried to do the impossible: replace his child's will with his own. It's a transplant that will never take. The moment hockey stops being a game, it's work. Who wants more work?

Micah told me that Coach Hendrix was a screamer on the bench, but I thought he was exaggerating.

"He's a rent-a-cop," I told Micah. "He's paid to keep it together."

"I know," said Micah. "That's what's so weird. He's like two different people. He's one kind of guy with parents but a completely different kind of guy with kids."

I paid close attention to Coach Hendrix after that. I watched him at practices but saw nothing. Then came a game in Brunswick, a prep school in Greenwich, Connecticut. It was one of those early mornings when even coffee doesn't help. There was a mist on the quad when we arrived. The campus was deserted. We parked and walked through empty halls, looking for the rink. In the lobby, we examined pictures of the oldest prep hockey teams. Every coach looked like Warren G. Harding. Most of the kids looked like George H. W. Bush. Every team had at least one ne'er-do-well, a mischievous trickster who you just knew died in the Argonne Forest or at the Battle of the Bulge. The equipment has improved, the game is faster, but important things have not changed. As the Green Bay Packer Max McGee said, "When it's third and ten, you can take the milk drinkers and I'll take the whiskey drinkers every time."

Coach Pete pulled me aside in the lobby. He said, "Coach Rizzo can't make it. Can you handle the defensive-side door?"

And that's how I came to see the other side of Coach Hendrix. He began screaming as soon as the puck dropped. He did not yell at any particular player, but at the team in general. He shouted what sounded less like specific instructions—"Center the puck!" "Cover the point!"—than like abstract concepts. His phrases were akin to modern paintings that have numbers instead of names. "Where's the ambition?" "Is your hair on fire?" "Are you a player?" I stared at him in surprise, but he did not seem to notice. He was wearing his Bears baseball hat and his Bears jacket with his name on the sleeve: "Coach Alan." He chewed a coffee stirrer, eyes like pinholes. The air around him dripped invective. *Shirker! Crap pass! Stupid play!* I was mesmerized. At times, lost in the moment, I forgot to open the defensive-side door, and the kids lined up, waiting to get off the ice.

"Hey, Coach," Coach Pete called to me, smiling. "Your job. The door."

It was a close game. The action went back and forth. I tried to catch Micah's eye, but he looked away. Over time, the nature of Coach Hendrix's invective changed. It went from fiery but abstract to concrete and harsh. He was yelling at specific players by the middle of the second, screaming till his voice was hoarse. "Duffy! Keep your fuckin' stick down! This ain't a prison yard." "Hey, Tommy! We all know you can skate. How about playing hockey!" His daughter got the worst of it. "Hey, Jenny! What the hell? Are you trying to embarrass me? I didn't raise you like that!"

Some parents see only the good when their kids play hockey. Coach Hendrix saw only the bad, the flaws, the smallest mistake or loss of concentration. Every lapse fell on him like a physical blow. He redirected his dismay and pain onto the narrow shoulders of Broadway Jenny, who skated faster and faster and chugged harder and harder but would never be good enough. By the third period, Coach Hendrix's diatribe, which had been intermittent, became a Joycean stream, a never-ending sentence in which the words were connected by hyphens. "Goddamnit-Jenny-what's-your-major-malfunction-the-puck-was-right-in-front-of-you!"

We were down by one with five minutes to go. Tommy stole the puck and skated up ice with Broadway Jenny, a two-on-one. (Brunswick had been caught changing lines, leaving them momentarily shorthanded.) They passed back and forth, back and forth. Tommy faked a shot—the goalie slid to cover—then passed to Broadway Jenny. She held the puck for what seemed like—*one* one thousand, *two* one thousand— two full seconds, then shot high, sailing the puck over an empty net. Her eyes were red when she got back to the bench. She sat next to her father, who had stopped yelling, who had stopped talking altogether. Ominous silence. His arms were crossed. He stared ahead. He leaned down and whispered to his daughter. She started sobbing. The other kids stole a glance at her, then looked away.

"Oh, stop it," said Coach Hendrix. "This is hockey."

I stared at him. He met my gaze, then said, "I'm not a hugger."

I looked at Coach Pete. He kept his eyes on the ice.

Broadway Jenny did not miss a shift. She was back out there a minute later, charging across the ice, hurling herself into the corners, redoubling her effort, as if this time she'd finally get it right.

Coach Pete pulled Dan with a minute left. Micah went on as the extra skater. He wore a plastic shield instead of a cage, which gave him the look of the boy in the bubble, closed off from the fury of the world. He got the puck inside the blue line, made a move, then carried it behind the net. He stood there with ten seconds to go. He waited a beat, then passed to Barry, who was rushing the goalie. What's more important? The pass or the shot? Barry snapped off a hard wrister and won the game.

I called Ralph Rizzo that night to ask about Coach Hendrix.

"Is he always like that?" I asked.

"Yeah, man. He gets into it. He goes a little far sometimes, but his heart's in the right place."

When I spoke to Coach Pete a few days later, he said the same thing.

"What he's doing to his daughter isn't right," I said.

"I hear you," said Coach Pete, "but it's his kid."

LAKE PLACID—AN INTERLUDE

An engraving from 1796 shows men on skates playing a game that looks like ice hockey on the frozen Thames in London. British soldiers played the same game on the Saint Lawrence River while stationed in Canada in the nineteenth century. Trappers carried it west, where they played on lakes and ponds amid old-growth evergreen forests. At first, they used a ball. They later switched to a wooden disk. On the frontier, the game was rough. Some players lost teeth. Others were knocked senseless and sat dumbstruck beneath the winter sun, wondering, "Who am I? Why am I here?" For most, it was a diversion. For a few, it became a passion. Because it was played on rivers that ribboned the North Woods, it was linked to the freedom and romance of the New World. Some called it "shinny." Some called it "hockey." It's been said to descend from lacrosse, football, even golf, but its adherents knew that it was its own game, with its own dangers, ethics, and code. It's the only major sport played someplace other than dry land. In North America, it's an example of man adapting to a hostile environment, a winter world of violence, teamwork, triumph, and pain.

The first indoor game was played on March 3, 1875, at the Victoria Skating Rink in Montreal. The teams—McGill University students—played nine to a side. Some positions in evidence that day (center, wing) remain familiar, while others (roamer, broom) have been forgotten. There were enough teams in Canada by 1883 to stage the first "championship" as part of Montreal's Winter Carnival. Within a few years, the winner of this tournament was being given a large silver punch bowl purchased for the occasion by Lord Stanley of Preston, who fell in love with hockey soon after he was appointed governor general of Canada by Queen Victoria in 1888. This cup, or one of its descendants—there have been three Stanley Cups—has been given to the world's best hockey team ever since.

There were a hundred Canadian hockey teams by 1900. Many of the standout players can be seen in photos at the Hockey Hall of Fame in Toronto. They wear wool sweaters and skimpy pads and primitive-looking skates. The first pro league was created in the United States. That's what America is for: inventing the market and making it pay. Called the International Professional Hockey League, it collapsed in 1907, only to be followed by other leagues that formed and dissolved, culminating with the founding of the National Hockey League in 1917. The NHL's early years were marked by the rise and fall of franchises, their names redolent of a lost age: the Vancouver Millionaires, the Seattle Metropolitans. By the 1940s, only a handful of clubs remained, the so-called Original Six: the New York Rangers, the Boston Bruins, the Montreal Canadiens, the Toronto Maple Leafs, the Chicago Blackhawks, and the Detroit Red Wings. Considered a golden age, the six-team era lasted until the league's first expansion in

1967. There are currently thirty-two NHL teams, with clubs in such unlikely cities as Miami, Phoenix, and Las Vegas.

The early days were marked by innovation, but the game settled into an equilibrium in the six-team era. This is hockey as I knew it in the 1970s. Dump and chase: the center dumps the puck into the corner, and the wing chases it, digs it out, and throws it in front of the net, where the center and the other wing try to bang it past the goalie. The object is to keep the puck in the other team's zone. Now and then, there'd be a breakaway, or you might live to see a genius like Bobby Orr, but for the most part, nothing much changed. The game we played was like slot hockey on ice, with each player stuck in his groove.

The stars of the NHL, as well as the team owners and announcers, believed there was no other way to play the game. Fans believed that no one in the world was playing it half as well. We knew about the Russians, of course—they were targeting us with nukes. We spent every minute watching for missile shadows. But we did not think much of their hockey. Russia, with its frozen steppe and endless winters, is God-given shinny country, but the Soviets got serious about the game only in the 1950s, when every sporting event came to be seen as a theater in the cold war. If the Russians got good fast, credit coach Anatoli Tarasov, who took control of the program in 1958. The Russian national team was part of the Red Army. Tarasov did not have to worry about recruiting players—he could simply have top prospects drafted. That's where the dictatorship of the proletariat has it all over capitalism. The fact that Tarasov did not grow up with the game turned out to be another plus. He came to it with what Buddhists call "beginner's mind," open and eager, a problem-solver

unencumbered by old habits. He built his team in the style of
Russian folkways, influenced less by dump and chase than by
the Bolshoi Ballet. To him, players were like gears in a machine. You did not pass to a teammate. You moved the puck
to the place the cog would be when the wheel turned. What's
more, while North American players, needing to make money
to support their families—the average NHL salary was
$17,934 in 1960—spent the off-season selling insurance or
pumping gas, the Soviets, being lieutenants and majors, were
able to train in a season without end. NHL players returned
from the summer with love handles and beer guts and had to
spend the first months of the season working their way back
into shape. The Russians were never in anything but perfect
condition. A typical NHL player might have taken a class and
earned a license so he could sell real estate or life insurance in
the off-season. The Russian's Boris Mayorov took up juggling
so he could improve his stick handling.

By the 1960s, the Russians had crafted a unique style.
Whereas the Canadians went up and down the ice—north to
south; dump to chase—the Soviets traveled every which way,
north to south, east to west, side to side, advancing, retreat-
ing, feinting, following an orbit that took them everywhere.
It seemed counterintuitive. If the object is to score, shouldn't
the players rush the goalie? But Tarasov, not knowing any
better, built his scheme on misdirection, with players spiraling, probing, searching for a weakness. It violated the old
rules. The Russians carried the puck in front of their own net,
went back and forth across the blue line as if it wasn't even
there, forsook a good shot believing a better shot would come.
This was about teamwork, speed, strategy. Dump and chase
was based on a simple idea—give up the puck, then get it

back. That made no sense to Tarasov. Why would you give up possession? The Soviets never willingly relinquished the puck.

When the Red Army started beating North American amateurs, no one thought much of it. The Soviet team was the equivalent of North American professionals, the best in their nation, men in their twenties and thirties. In the capitalist West, amateurs really were amateurs: unpaid college kids or those not good enough for the big leagues. We believed that any halfway decent NHL team—the 1966–67 Rangers, say, who finished 30–28–12—would annihilate the Russians.

In the summer of 1972, a team of Canadian All-Stars played an eight-game series against the Red Army. It was called the Summit Series. Team Canada included many of the best players in the NHL: Bobby Orr, Bobby Clarke, Stan Mikita, Phil Esposito, and Ken Dryden, who published the diary he kept during the match as *Face-off at the Summit*. Every fan figured it would be a blowout, a schooling for the Commies. Team Canada did in fact score just thirty seconds into game one. "Phil Esposito tapped a rebound past [the Russian goalie] Tretiak," Dryden wrote. "I felt pretty confident. Then we scored again. Bobby Clarke clearly won a face-off to Tretiak's right, drew the puck back to Paul Henderson, and he scored. Tretiak never moved on Paul's shot. Two goals in less than seven minutes."

To fans—the game was played before eighteen thousand at the Montreal Forum—it looked like the expected cakewalk, but the players knew better. The fact is, the Canadians, many of whom were still in "summer shape," could not keep up with the spinning gyre. It was more than just conditioning: Team Canada was a collection of All-Stars—these guys had never played together. The Red Army had been working as a unit for a dozen years. They functioned like a machine. "They started to pass the puck with beautiful combinations," wrote Dryden. "There was Yevgeny Zimin banging one in from the crease. Goal. 2–1. Then they began playing keep-away with the puck."

The Red Army tied the score at the end of the first period and went on to win the game 7–3, sending the Canadian populace into shock. "It was a really interesting game," Dryden wrote. "You learn only when you lose."

The Canadians battled back, winning several games, but this was clearly not going to be easy. The series then shifted to Russia. ("I slept for about an hour in the airport, woke up, started to read James Dickey's *Deliverance*, and then decided to buy a camera at the duty-free shop," Dryden reported.) The games were played at the Palace of Sports in Moscow, where, according to Dryden, "the big three of Soviet politics—Leonid Brezhnev, Alexei Kosygin and Nikolai Podgorny—sat in the presidential box, while Yevgeny Yevtushenko, the great poet, was practically in the rafters."

The series came down to the final minute of the final game, which Team Canada won with thirty-four seconds left in regulation—Esposito shot, Henderson got the rebound and scored. And though Canada won, they lost something, too—that aura of invincibility. "It took us about ten minutes to realize the Canadian professionals are ordinary human beings, like us," one of the Russians said. The Red Army only got better. They won the Olympic gold in 1964, 1968, 1972, and 1976. By 1980, they'd come to be seen as a kind of dark star, the unbeatable hockey monolith from beyond the sun.

The United States won gold in hockey at the 1960 Olympics in Squaw Valley, California, but it seemed like a fluke.

Compared with Russia and Canada, America was a shinny backwater. We were the land of baseball, football, basketball. Hockey was less sibling to these sports than first or even second cousin. Few American players had ever been good enough to play in the NHL. There were just fourteen in the league in 1970. It was closer to twenty-one by 1980, still a distinct minority, and most of them were barely hanging on. That's why the success of the 1980 U.S. Olympic hockey team was considered a miracle. The squad, coached by the University of Minnesota's Herb Brooks, consisted entirely of college kids. Fans can still recall certain names—Neal Broten, Jim Craig, Mike Eruzione—but even these were not great players. Only five of them went on to significant NHL careers. What the team had was strategy, chemistry, and timing, as well as a great coach. These were the bleak last days of the cold war—act 5, scene 10—a time of hostages and mullahs, stagflation and ICBMs.

Team USA beat teams they had no business beating at Lake Placid. Czechoslovakia, Norway, Sweden. Then, on February 22, 1980, a day inscribed in the heart of every American hockey fan, they beat the Russian national team. The final score was 4–3. Millions of us remember where we were when the news came. The game was shown on tape delay—it was played in the afternoon, but the network held it for prime time—but word leaked. In Chicago, the sports anchor threw his blue cards in the air and screamed, "We're not supposed to say, but I can't keep the secret. We won! We won! We beat the Commies!" Many of us still remember the go-ahead goal, which came in the middle of the third period. A Team USA defenseman dumped the puck into the Russian corner. It ricocheted, bouncing back along the boards, where another

American, a forward seeking to corral it, fell down as he redirected the puck to center ice, and that's where Mike Eruzione picked it up. A little older than the others, Eruzione was the team's chunky, dark-haired, hardworking captain—his college teammates called him "Pete Rose on skates." Eruzione, a bartender's son raised in Winthrop, Massachusetts, the captain of his high school team and a Boston University standout, got the puck at center ice, twenty feet from the Russian goal. He took three strides, leaned in, then shot around a Russian defender, using him to create a screen. The Russian goalie Vladimir Myshkin never got a good look. The puck was in the back of the net before he knew what was happening.

The Russians attacked wildly in the last minutes of the game—like a struck shark, they flailed in their own blood. The arena erupted when the horn sounded. The Americans skated wildly toward their goalie, Jim Craig. The United States, as a prospect and an experiment, probably should have ended at that moment. Fold up the tent, send home the clowns. It would never feel that good again. It was like we'd won a war. As the Russians skated away in defeat, the Soviet Union began to collapse—that's how it felt anyway. Repercussions followed: as hundreds of thousands of Americans enlisted in the army the day after Pearl Harbor was attacked, hundreds of thousands now signed their kids up for hockey. Thus the modern era was born. There are currently 174 U.S. citizens playing in the NHL, including several of the league's best players. Micah, his teammates, and all their opponents are the children of that moment.

The Herb Brooks Arena at Lake Placid has been sanctified as a result. It's a shrine visited by fans who want to see the site of the miracle. It's like the Grotto in Lourdes, France, where

Bernadette witnessed an apparition of the Virgin Mary, only instead of the Virgin Mary, it was Herb Brooks, and instead of healing—many are healed by the waters at Lourdes—it's the power of hockey past.

The most beloved tournament of the FCAH season is staged by Can/Am—an international company that's been producing standout hockey tournaments for over fifty years—in Lake Placid each November, with hundreds of players from dozens of teams changing in the same locker rooms and skating on the same ice as the heroes of 1980.

This would be Micah's third trip to Lake Placid, though for him, unlike for me, it never gets old. I picked him up from school early Friday afternoon. Who cares if a kid misses a few hours of sixth grade? I parked behind the fleet of school buses dozing in anticipation of the afternoon rush. It was November early in the third millennium. Donald Trump was tweeting. The nation was losing its mind. Hockey had not changed.

Micah's jerseys, sticks, and equipment bag were in the trunk. We stopped for coffee, candy, petrol, then headed north. We took Route 7 to I-84, then got on the Taconic State Parkway, which, like a glade in a fairy tale, is lovely—the parkway winds through Rip Van Winkle country, beautiful but spiked with danger. There are drunk drivers, texters, cell phone talkers. It's easy to drift into a trance on that road—highway hypnosis. Before you know it, you're going much too fast. In a terrible premonition, you see your car in flames at the bottom of a gorge.

Cops hide in every blind on the Taconic, aching to ruin your day. When wet, the pavement turns into Mylar. When cold, it turns into ice. Micah peppered me with questions. I could not tell if he really wanted to know these things or just liked the sound of conversation. His questions led to other questions until, now and then, I'd ask myself how I'd ended up talking about string theory, the Iran hostage crisis, or why statistics can't explain the greatness of Jackie Robinson. Micah favors either/or inquiries about life in general. "If you had a choice of being a very successful lawyer who made millions of dollars *or* a baseball player who got to the majors but played in very few games and only as a pinch runner, which would you choose?" "If you could be a great hockey player with a short career or a good hockey player with a long career, which would it be?" A lot of his questions are about God and the afterlife. "If an old man dies, will he be old in heaven?" "If a person has used evil to make the world a better place, will he go to hell?" When Judd Meese drove Micah to an away game, his "we made it safely" email told me he'd gotten the business: "We made it in under two hours, the game was great, and the whole way back Micah and Barry talked about God. I'll say this: they are not well informed."

I am particular about music on such trips, toggling between a handful of satellite stations, playing the Beatles, Tom Petty, Frank Sinatra singing "Nice 'n' Easy": "We're on the road to romance—that's safe to say / but let's make all the stops along the way." I instruct my son with my selections, tell him, "These are the things of *my* world. You can accept or reject them. Either way will work."

We exited at Route 73, which narrows as it climbs into the Adirondacks. The mountains are ancient, the peaks beaten down by the wind and water of geologic time. The rounded summits are carpeted with fir trees. At its apex, the range stands over five thousand feet, pint-size compared with the western mountains, but awesome up close. Route 73 crosses a valley on its final approach to Lake Placid. Waterfalls and cliffs on this side, frozen lakes on that. I turned off the music and opened the windows. We could hear the Ausable River. The air was cold and clean. You know you've made it when you start seeing motels and restaurants, then the old Olympic architecture, the ski jump and training complexes. The main drag is called Sentinel Road. It was lit up when we arrived, crowded with cars and people. The distant mountains had become a black line against a dark blue sky. The stars were out. Sirius was blazing. The temperature had dropped to fifteen degrees.

We were staying with half a dozen other youth hockey teams at the Crowne Plaza on top of a hill above the commercial strip. You could see the town from the windows, the lake, and the distant shore. The lobby was crawling with hockey players of every age, size, and demeanor trailed by every variety of coach. You could draw a map of the Northeast and the mid-Atlantic by looking at the jackets: the Lexington-Bedford Barons, the Malvern Ice Eagles, the Montclair Hitmen, the New City Rascals, the Kent Stars, the Cape Cod Lobstermen, the Medford Storm, the Portsmouth Pilgrims, the Portland Progress. The parents were already drinking at the bar.

The desk clerk gave us a list of rules when we checked in. These had clearly been devised in response to previous incidents. He asked Micah to read the list out loud, then drew special attention to rule fourteen: "I will not participate in the game known as knee hockey, which is played by children on their knees with shortened sticks and a small hockey net, in any public areas of the hotel, including but not limited to meeting rooms, dining rooms and restaurants, the pool deck, fitness area, business center, and guest hallways."

When asked if he understood rule fourteen, Micah nodded.

"I need verbal consent," said the clerk.

"Yes," said Micah. "I understand."

We were among the last Bears to arrive, which is why we ended up in the handicapped room beside the elevator. There was only one bed, a double. We went to sleep on opposite sides but always woke up together, hugging for warmth.

Micah left in search of his teammates as soon as he'd dumped his bags. I followed. There is a toy store in Lake Placid that sells wooden rubber-band guns. Some have been made to look like pistols, some like rifles, some like machine guns. The most elaborate model shoots fifty rubber bands at once, a killing fusillade. The hotel halls were filled with gun-toting kids. They'd pop out of the shadows, look you up and down, then wave you through. Now and then, you'd hear a distant rumble and think, "I'm glad I'm not over there."

I tried to sit with several other parents who'd camped in deck chairs beside the indoor pool, but the air was too steamy and chlorine-soaked. Pee Wees packed the Jacuzzi. More parents were eating dinner at the buffet, which started with chicken-fried steak and ended with a crescendo of fluorescent gelatin squares. The parents divided into cliques, like high school. There were the ins and the outs, the blessed and the damned. Status came from your child. If he could play, you were in. If he could not play, you ate alone. The damned returned to their rooms after dinner, while the blessed lingered in the bar.

I took a seat beside Simone Camus, the Pee Wee parent at the bottom of the social ladder. Her status was partly due to a particular episode. Whereas most parents brought beer coolers or coffee thermoses to games, Simone brought a crystal pitcher filled with iced tea. One afternoon, she placed it beside her on a bench in the Winter Garden, where Broadway Jenny caught it with her stick. It shattered, sending glass and tea everywhere. Coach Hendrix scolded his daughter—"How many times have I told you to watch your stick!"—then apologized and helped Simone clean up the mess. He thought that was the end of it, but a week later Simone sent a bill for $250. When Coach Hendrix realized this was not a joke, he flew into a rage—"Who brings a crystal vase to a hockey rink?"—and refused to pay. Simone persisted; he ignored her. So here she was, outcast, as far from Paris as a person can get.

Micah went out with his knee hockey stuff after dinner. I reminded him about rule fourteen, but he didn't listen. I could hear him playing in the hall with teammates, shouting and cheering. Someone was flung into a wall. Then it got quiet. An adult was talking. The man from reception. He'd handed one of the kids the rules and made him read rule fourteen out loud. I could hear a small voice. I think it was Tommy. "I will not participate in the game known as knee hockey, which is played by children on their knees with shortened sticks and a small hockey net, in any public areas of the hotel, including but not limited to meeting rooms, dining rooms and restaurants, the pool deck, fitness area, business center, and guest hallways."

"Where are you?" asked the man from reception.

"Planet Earth," said Tommy.

"In a public hallway on planet Earth," the man corrected. "Please return to your rooms, or your equipment will be confiscated."

Micah came in a moment later.

When I asked him what had happened, he said, "Nothing."

The Bears played their first game at seven the next morning. The Herb Brooks Arena is on the main drag across from Mirror Lake. There are three rinks inside, jerry-rigged together. The complex is packed with waiting areas, hallways, locker rooms. There's a skate-sharpening station, a gift shop, and a nurse's office. The oldest rink was built for the 1930 Olympics, which were also played at Lake Placid. Canada took gold that year, followed by Weimar Germany and Switzerland. America did not finish in the top ten. Even Imperial Japan beat us. The 1930 rink is elegantly old-fashioned, with seats climbing up to a barrel roof. There's a practice rink, which is small and gritty, with just a handful of seats for parents; then there's the 1980 rink, where the miracle happened. It's state of the art circa the Carter administration, a cavernous hall distinguished by the huge four-sided scoreboard that hangs over center ice. It's the permanent home of the Adirondack Thunder, a minor-league team.

A TV outside each rink plays *Miracle*, Hollywood's take on the 1980 triumph, on a continuous loop. I always seemed to pass by during the penultimate scene, in which Herb Brooks, played by Kurt Russell, talks to his squad before the Russian game: "Great moments are born from great opportunity," he says. "And that's what you have here tonight, boys. That's what you've earned here tonight. One game. If we played them ten times, they might win nine. But not this game, not tonight. Tonight we skate with them. Tonight we stay with them. And we shut them down because we can. Tonight we are the greatest hockey team in the world. You were born to be hockey players. Every one of you. And you were meant to be here tonight. This is your time. Their time is done. It's over. I'm sick and tired of hearing about what a great hockey team the Soviets have. Screw 'em. This is your time. Now, go out there and take it."

Outside each locker room is a name of the team that used it during the 1980 Olympics: Team Sweden, Team Norway, Team Canada. The American locker room is the best to change in, but dressing where the Russians got lectured by their coach after the upset is pretty cool, too.

The Pee Wee A Bears started the tournament on the practice rink. I was pressed to the Plexiglas near our goal when the puck was dropped to start the game against the Duxbury, Massachusetts, Ducks. I'd been giving Micah pep talks all year. I might say, "Look for the pass, take the shot." Or "Use your body on the boards." I kept it simple in Lake Placid: "Skate hard, have fun."

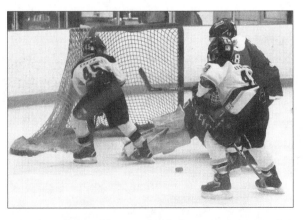

Crashing the net. There is no such thing as a garbage goal.

And it worked. Micah was a demon on the first shift, chasing pucks, skating down opponents. He set up in front of Duxbury's net, making himself a nuisance to the goalie, who pushed and wacked till given a penalty. Micah developed a new style at Lake Placid. He became an agitator. "He's mediocre when he lollygags," Coach Pete told me later, "but he's an impact player when he goes crazy." The romance of the location kicked the entire team into higher gear. The Bears played with hustle all weekend.

They were even better that afternoon and the next morning. They passed the puck, crowded the goalie, took a lot of shots, scored a lot of goals. They beat Portland, Cape Cod, Potomac, Montclair. It was turning into a breakthrough weekend. Something like this happened every year at Lake Placid. Maybe it was being away from home, staying together in a hotel—the kids were becoming a team.

The peak came in the middle of the tournament. We had to beat the Vikings from Haverhill, Massachusetts, to make the gold-medal round. We were down 4–1 at the end of the first. That's when the Bears usually rolled over to have their bellies rubbed, but this time was different. They kept plugging, passing, shooting, pressuring the goalie. They kept *trying*. Tommy McDermott tied the game late in the third period with a laser from beyond the hash marks. The game-winner came a minute later. Tommy again, sailing a slap shot from the blue line. It went over the net, hit the boards, and bounced back to Barry, who got it in front of an empty net. He waited a moment, toying with the goalie, then finished the play.

"That's it," said Jerry Sherman, slapping me on the back. "We're in."

All the Pee Wee players gathered at the hotel banquet

room that night for a party, meaning pizza and pop. Can/Am, the hosts of the tournament, had put together a highlight reel showing every goal and standout play from the weekend. The kids watched themselves as they ate, commenting and heckling. "Look at that toe drag!" "What a save!" They were like surfers, crowded into a Malibu cottage, watching themselves on Super 8, validated in a way that only film can validate.

Though they hadn't had alcohol, the kids seemed hungover as they sat in the Russian locker room the next morning preparing for the gold-medal game. The 1980 Rink, the Sunday before Thanksgiving. Coach Pete made them run through the parking lot, hoping the cold air would wake them up. Dark clouds in the distance. A single snowflake fell. I remember thinking, "That's the first snowflake of winter." Ten minutes later, we were in a snow globe.

Once dressed, the kids stood along the Plexiglas, watching the last minutes of the concession game—the team that came in third place won a bronze medal. Tournament veterans said it was better to win the concession game than to go down in the championship, in which case you'd get the silver medal but finish the weekend with a loss.

I was leaning against a wall in the lobby as Coach Hendrix talked Coaches Wilson and Rizzo through his scouting report on the Lexington-Bedford Barons, the team we'd play for gold. He broke down each Baron by number and position, describing one as dirty, another as crafty, a third as dumb. He said, "They are beatable, but the key is our second line. Their best players are better than our best, and our worst players are worse than their worst, but we have an edge in the middle."

Dozens of kids from the other teams—the teams that had been eliminated—had stuck around to watch the gold-medal game. The Ridgefield Bantams and Midgets, who would play after us, came to watch, too, as did rink rats and Can/Am officials. It gave the game a feel of genuine importance. The Pee Wee As went back to the locker room while the ice was resurfaced by not one but *two* Zambonis working in tandem—that's big time.

Coach Pete spoke to the kids, then led the way to the tunnel, where we could see them silhouetted in dim stadium light. The players were introduced one at a time. As each skated out, the scoreboard flashed a picture and stats: height, weight, favorite athlete, and favorite song. Barry Meese: 5'2", 103 lb., Patrick Kane, "Crazy Train." Jean Camus: 5'2", 105 lb., Brad Marchand, "Sweet Child O' Mine."

The Lexington-Bedford Barons, who had not lost at the tournament, came out like stone-faced killers. This one with a sneer, that one with a mullet, this one with a scar, that one with fresh stitches. None was under five feet tall, nor less than a hundred pounds, which, converted from Pee Wee to NHL, equals 6'4", 220. They executed precise drills during warm-ups. You could hear their freshly sharpened blades cutting the ice. It was like a commercial for Ginsu knives. The Bears appeared to be a rabble in comparison, a mismatched collection of height and weight. Not even our jerseys matched—some parents had bought new sweaters in the off-season while others stood pat. Micah had been wearing the same jersey for years. It was a relic, a rare example of an abandoned design. His name was written in a different font from the others'. He wore it differently, too, tucked in in back, like Gretzky.

The Bears looked lost in the early minutes. It was their first game on the Olympic-size ice, which is significantly bigger than the standard North American rink—200 by 100 feet compared to 200 by 85 feet, fifteen feet wider. They never got used to it. They'd slow down where the boards would normally be, dumbstruck at how the ice continued on.

You can tell a lot about a place by its hockey parents. Lexington and Bedford are affluent towns outside Boston, filled with professors and economists, doctors, biologists and engineers. It skews upper-middle class and Asian. Many of these parents, who sat together across the aisle, wore Patagonia coats or Burberry jackets, tweed pants, loafers. They had the air of overachievers, believers in the meritocracy. They worked hard, as did their children. Their kids would prevail because it's what they deserved. To win all the games only to lose in the final did not make sense. It's not just that they wanted their kids to beat our kids; they counted on it. They also had an overdeveloped sense of decorum. Every time one of our kids slashed or threw an elbow, one of their parents would tsk-tsk the Ridgefield side as if to ask, "Did you teach them to play like that?"

The Barons scored seventy-two seconds into the first period. Dan had not even settled in. Early goals are often the coach's fault. He's failed to prepare his team for the onslaught, failed to communicate something important. An early goal can crush the spirit. A few minutes later, they scored again, a kid from the Barons putting the puck between Dan's legs—the five-hole. The kid said something to the players on our bench as he skated past. I did not hear it—Micah later said he called them "pussies"—but I saw how our kids reacted. It woke them up. That's when they started to play.

I got a good look at Micah's face in the second period. It was sweaty, happy, and beet red. He was pressuring a Lexington-

Bedford kid, who, hurried into action, flung the puck away. Micah slid in front, and the puck hit his kneepad. You could hear the thunk in the bleachers. The puck bounced. Micah chased it, got it, and went up ice. A defender pushed him to the outside. This being Olympic ice, he skated and skated, carrying the puck around the net, then set up behind the goalie. The defense backed off, anticipating a pass. Micah looked at his center, Patrick Campi, then skated around and shot instead. A minute later, Micah's name was announced over the loudspeaker. "Goal, number forty-five, Micah Cohen."

The game was tied at two with a minute left in the third period. Cowbells, air horns, kazoos—the Lexington-Bedford parents were on their feet, wild with anticipation. Their entire team had crashed our net and were trying to jam in the winner. Dan slid this way and that, making save after save. He wanted to corral the puck and get a whistle, but it kept slipping away. The Barons had already blown two good chances, but were going to score—you could feel it.

Then the moment arrived. Dan was out of position; the puck, having pinged off Brian Rizzo's skate, spun like a top in our crease, a foot from our empty net. There were three things in the world: the Lexington-Bedford center, the puck, the goal line. As the Lexington-Bedford kid tried to finish the play, Barry dove onto the ice and covered the puck with his hand. Everyone jumped on top of Barry, creating a pile. The whistle blew.

Barry had committed a penalty. No one but the goalie is allowed to cover the puck. It should have resulted in a penalty shot, but the ref either did not see it, or did not want the game to end that way. When the Lexington-Bedford parents realized there'd be no call, they booed. They called us names and spoke to us sarcastically: "Congratulations, Ridgefield. You have taught your children very well. They are the very best. The very best cheaters."

Sharon Rizzo said, "Oh my."

Simone Camus said, "*Mon Dieu.*"

Parents on both sides started shouting at each other. I was right in the middle of it, screaming with the rest. Then something happened.

My father used to tell me about his migraines and the aura that preceded them, the loss of eyesight and the sense of precognition, nausea, and pain. I did not think much of it till sophomore year in college when, while sitting in a writing workshop, my vision went spotty, as if I'd been staring into the sun. When I looked at my classmates, their faces disassembled, broke into pieces. Everything was like a Picasso. Not a face but a nose, an ear, an iris—a blue iris. I did not feel bad, but actually sort of good. Buzzy, giddy. My soul had been freed from my body and, free from my body, realized the things my body had been furiously engaged in were in fact stupid. The plans, motivations, worries—stupid, stupid, stupid. I found that, in this state, I could see everything in my life with detachment, as if from a distance. When I called my mom to tell her I had a brain tumor, she said, "No, you've got a migraine, like your father."

No one knows what causes migraines. Triggers vary. For some, it's stress. For others, it's chocolate. For some, it's youth hockey. That's what I learned in the last seconds of the gold-medal game at Lake Placid. My vision fractured and my soul drifted above, then, looking down on the scene, said, "What are you doing? Why do you care! This is all so stupid! You will live and die and none of this will have mattered. The only thing that matters is Micah—not his skill level, not his play-

ing time or status on this team. Just Micah. Your child."
Looking around at the screaming parents, I suddenly felt like
a sober person amid a crowd of roaring drunks.

That's when I actually began to enjoy the game, which had
gone into overtime. Sudden death. There'd be a five-minute
period of three-on-three hockey. If that ended in a tie, the
game would continue for five minutes of two-on-two hockey,
followed, if necessary, by one-on-one hockey played until one
side scored.

Coach Pete sent Tommy, Brian, and Joey out for the first
minute of OT—one forward, two defensemen. Micah went
out with Barry and Broadway Jenny for the next thirty seconds. Judd Meese sat next to me, keeping score. Sue Campi
had broken her own rule and gone for a fourth beer. Tommy's
father was laughing with delight. His wife, Eunice, was praying at his side: "Dear Lord, bring our boys and our girls the
success they have worked so hard for."

Living large in Lake Placid

The buzzer sounded and the game went into a second overtime—two-on-two. Tommy and Joey, the stepbrothers, started it and finished it, skating together beautifully, a healing thing to watch. A minute into that overtime, with the spectators on their feet and the noisemakers wailing, Tommy skated toward our own zone with the puck, chased by two Barons, who, in this way, left Joey uncovered. Tommy flung the puck backward down ice without looking. Joey gathered it, turned, took two strides, and shot. It hit the top post and went straight into the goal—this is called "bar down." And that was it. Game over.

The rest of the Bears jumped over the boards and sprinted across the ice, throwing off helmets and gloves like Team USA at the end of *Miracle*. Dan Arcus pushed his mask onto his forehead and leaned against the crossbar, grinning. To be a goalie, to withstand the fury amid teammates and yet remain alone . . . what must these young netminders be like in later life, when, as bankers and lawyers, they are surrounded by people who have no idea who they really were or what they had accomplished?

The Barons cried in the handshake line. Our kids were crying, too. Win or lose, the emotion of the weekend overwhelms. A red carpet was rolled across the ice, a podium set up. A Can/Am official talked about the importance of competition and sportsmanship. The medals were presented—silver and gold—with a captain from each team standing on a platform. There was a torch. It went hand to hand. For a moment, I thought it was going to set one of the Pee Wees ablaze. The players skated over one at a time to collect their medals. Barry pumped a fist as he went, then raised his medal skyward. Tommy went down the line of teammates, shoving cheap cigars into various mouths. These were confiscated by Coach Hendrix, but not before Tommy got off a plume of blue smoke. Micah kissed his medal as he'd seen players kiss the Stanley Cup. A picture of this—Micah kissing the gold—would later appear on the cover of *Can/Am* magazine.

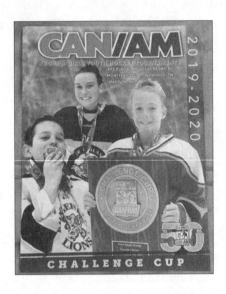

It was snowing when we got out of the rink. The roads had not been cleared. It made for treacherous driving. I descended in low gear. The river had frozen, the waterfalls stopped. It had been autumn when we'd arrived in Lake Placid; now it was winter. That tournament always feels like a turning point, a hockey equinox. Some players who started out strong would fade after Lake Placid. These were hothouse flowers, not built for the long haul. Others emerged. The season is endless. To succeed, you have to enjoy the grind. It took us an hour to get down to the highway. The snowplows were out in force by then, blasting tunnels through the storm. It was all flurries and headlights on the Taconic. Micah wore his medal all the way home. I could see him in the rearview mirror dozing with it around his neck.

I pulled over at the first McDonald's. The parking lot was nearly empty. An off-duty employee was smoking a cigarette in the storm. I ordered two Big Macs, then headed for the bathroom. And there was Parky, unshaven and alone at a table in back. The term "bedhead" does not do him justice. He was making his way through a stack of cheeseburgers. I approached cautiously, waiting for him to notice me. When he did, it was with a sad smile. His eyes were full of suffering. It was a pain I knew intimately, but would never admit to anyone with real problems. Hockey-parent pain. "My kid is getting hosed" pain.

"Where's Duffy?" I asked.

"Sleeping in the car, though God knows, he doesn't need it. He hardly played."

"Why do you think?" I asked.

"Rizzo hates him."

"Why?"

"Because he's better than Brian."

DECEMBER

Ridgefield has been the setting or the backdrop for many Christmas movies. It appears as "Bridgefield"—genius, that—in the 1939 Cary Grant movie *In Name Only*, which peaks with an unforgettable Christmas Eve scene, and seems present in half a dozen other movies from Hollywood's golden age, including *Mr. Blandings Builds His Dream House, The Lady Eve,* and *Christmas in Connecticut*. In 2017, it appeared on the Hallmark Channel in *Coming Home for Christmas*. Several sequences have been shot on Main Street. There is snow in these scenes, Christmas trees, debutantes. In other words, our town has long been depicted as the epitome of the holiday season. The brick houses and the strings of colored lights, the snow in the spruce trees, the dogs on the porches and the hot chocolate in the mugs—it's Christmas as imagined by Hollywood. Each decade brings a new population to town, and yet this vibe, which is older and stronger than any of us, remains.

Ridgefielders tend to be secular, mildly religious at most, yet the town is packed with faith institutions, each nurturing its own tradition and its own truth, each telling its own version of the biggest story. As of the most recent census, Ridgefield had 24,638 inhabitants. Nearly 30 percent of them were under eighteen years old—youth hockey age. About 15 percent were over sixty-five, meaning lots of grandparents to attend youth hockey games. The town covers thirty-five square miles. In that space, among that population, I counted one bookstore, one movie theater, three diners, one candy store, four ice-cream shops, and thirteen houses of worship: Jesse Lee Church, St. Mary's Roman Catholic, St. Stephen's Episcopal, St. Andrew's Lutheran, Ridgefield Baptist Congregation de Notre Dame, St. Elizabeth Seton, First Congregational Church, Ridgebury Congregational, the Ridgefield Christian Center, the First Church of Christ Scientist, Congregation Shir Shalom, the Chabad Jewish Center of Ridgefield, and Christ the King, an ornate cathedral that looks like it belongs on the Russian steppe. (Its congregants are schismatic, Catholics who reject Vatican II.) Do Ngak Kunphen Ling, a beautiful Buddhist temple, is just across the border in Redding.

All these institutions are packed in the weeks leading up to Christmas. It's the Frank Capra movie on TV, the candles in the windows, the lights in the spruce trees, the family talk in the supermarket, the snow and smell of snow in the wind, the puffy coats on the toddlers, the galoshes on the elderly, the carolers in Ballard Park, the junior high school concert, the playhouse spectacular. Even if it's not your holiday, you are driven toward transcendence. One day, I will go into every church, monastery, and synagogue in Ridgefield and ask each priest, minister, monk, and rabbi three simple questions: Who are we? Why are we here? What should we do?

No matter the denomination or faith, the people in this book share a religion: hockey. We go to games on Sunday mornings and call on the Lord in churchlike rinks across the Northeast. As in Christianity, December is a special time in hockey. This is when we break for two weeks, meaning two weeks of peace on earth and goodwill to men. Two weeks to watch football. Fourteen days to heal and remember. When it gets cold, families build makeshift rinks behind their houses, bumpy ice sheets surrounded by a patchwork of boards, a six-pack of Budweiser cooling in a snowbank. You can spend entire days rink hopping, going from house to house, playing under the floodlights, beneath the glowing stars. Snowflakes whirl out of the void. If it's very cold, the lakes and the rivers freeze. When it's cold without snow, the ponds turn into black mirrors. We park beneath the trees on such days, lace our skates in the car, then venture onto the ice with sticks and pucks. We skate for hours beneath the clouds and above the clouds, or, if the ice is exceptionally clear, above schools of fish. When you think of it later, it feels like a dream, hours on the ice, bewitched and between, passing a puck as you move from the lake to the river, then through the woods, with only the sound of wind and skate blades.

Hockey returned via email. It came as half a dozen plays sent not by Coach Pete but by Coach Hendrix. He said we were to have our kids memorize these plays, which, when I printed them out and looked them over, made no sense to me. They were super complicated, the sort an NHL team might deploy in the last minute of a playoff game. Hockey is not football. Few actions are choreographed. Mostly you just play. It's not music read from a sheet—it's jazz, a freewheeling improvisation. Everyone on the ice has a position and a role, but within that role, you are at liberty to follow the action. There are few stoppages in play, few occasions for a coach to intervene. In the best case, a game flows. You ride its energy like a wave. It's the game itself that dictates, not the coaches. A good player reads the wave and reacts. A great player anticipates and redirects. The few plays you do learn in advance (power play, penalty kill) are akin to a fast break in basketball—a template deployed in special circumstances. You get into it as a boxer gets into a stance. It tells you where to start but not where to end. But the Pee Wee A Bears had not even learned those basic templates. Our kids were unschooled at the direction of USA Hockey, a national organization that wants pre–high school-ers to forget about templates and diagrams and go, go, go. Coach Hendrix's plays went against that—they were lousy with arrows, dashes, and dotted lines. You could get a headache just looking at them.

It was a strange moment in the season. Coach Pete did not turn up for much of the month. It was like when Reagan got shot. There was a void. Coach Hendrix flowed into it as naturally as Al Haig. He was as exuberant as Haig, too, and no one was in the mood. A kid named Nico Mallozzi, who played for the Connecticut RoughRiders, had died a few weeks after Christmas. He'd not been well but went to a tournament anyway, toughness being a primary virtue in hockey. He'd sickened at a rink in Buffalo, New York, then died on the way home. He was ten years old. It was sepsis, a result of pneumonia. We played the RoughRiders a few weeks later. It was on temporary ice, beneath a tent in a park on Long Island Sound. The wind whipped off the water, snapping the canvas. The kids got changed in a trailer, then stood at the blue line before the game with their helmets off and heads bowed, observing a moment of silence for Nico Mallozzi. The puck was dropped, but neither team could focus on the game.

I overheard Barry Meese ask his father: "Why are we even playing?"

Coach Hendrix yelled at the kids between periods. He was throbbing with anger. We could hear him calling out individual players, demanding an explanation for their "half-ass effort."

"Where are your heads?" he demanded.

And so the Bears began the second part of their season in another funk—it was like a relapse, the recurrence of a bad mood. It had to do with Coach Pete's absence. I figured—who really knew?—he'd gone off to deal with his father's case, which I'd followed in the paper. Old Buck Wilson had been sentenced to six and a half years in a federal penitentiary. I suspected Coach Pete was needed at home, which is why he'd disappeared. When he did show up at one practice, he seemed diminished. The bounce was gone from his step. He was hangdog and looked older. We were a crew without a captain in those weeks, which allowed the mad, self-interested first mates (Rizzo, Hendrix) to take over, give orders, and chart a new course, turning us immediately into the wind. Coach Hendrix's plays were step one. Then the practices changed. What had been happy sessions dominated by scrimmages, shoot-outs, and relay races were now all about drills. "Who said hockey is supposed to be fun?" Coach Hendrix shouted through his whistle. "Skate!"

Though they worked together, Coaches Rizzo and Hendrix clearly had different objectives. Coach Rizzo wanted to develop his son, which meant getting him as much ice time as possible. He remade the defense to do this. What had been two units became a platoon, with Brian on the ice every other shift. In a forty-five-minute game, Brian Rizzo might play thirty-five minutes. Other kids were shortchanged as a result.

Coach Hendrix aimed for something similar, only it was his daughter Broadway Jenny he wanted to rebuild around. She'd been a top player in Mites and Squirts but had begun to fall behind. She was small and weak on her pins. Even a glancing blow sent her sprawling. She'd gotten by on hustle and hockey sense. It's not that she was working less—her legs were still driving like pistons—nor had she forgotten how to play, but the boys were getting bigger and stronger and more physical. While she stayed the same speed, they'd found another gear. That's why Coach Pete had moved her from center to right wing. Centers have to do the most skating, while a wing can cheat a bit, positioning himself or herself near the blue line at the start of the rush. Coach Hendrix could have dealt with this in a variety of ways. He could have accepted reality and prepared Jenny to be a center on an elite girls' team. He could have taught her to play wing properly—a smart wing can make up for a lack of speed by being in position. (You don't have to be as fast if you're waiting when the puck arrives.) He decided to remake our offense instead. We'd played with nine forwards divided into three lines. Coach Hendrix moved one of those players—Patrick Campi— to defense, then switched the others around. There'd now be three sets of wings and two centers, who'd double-shift, playing on every other line. Tommy would be one of the centers. Broadway Jenny would be the other. Coach Rizzo had Brian double-shifting. Coach Hendrix would do the same with Jenny.

Since the rush was too fast for Broadway Jenny, Coach Hendrix slowed it down. That's what was happening at practice; he was gumming up the works with plays and rules that would downshift the offense to a speed that better suited his daughter. The wings were no longer allowed to head up ice the moment the defense took possession of the puck. They now had to wait at the blue line so that Tommy or Jenny could lead the way. Of course, this is not what Hendrix told the parents. He told us that the hockey we'd been playing, the style that resulted in our gaudy win-loss record, was selfish and unsound.

"Flawed," he'd say. "Not good team hockey."

Several dispiriting snoozefests resulted, the sort of games even a loving parent can't stand to watch. When Duffy insisted on playing full speed, taking off with the puck alone, leaving Broadway Jenny behind, Coach Hendrix benched him.

"Until when?" asked Duffy.

"Until you learn to play team hockey," said Coach Hendrix.

We never scored more than twice a night. When we did win, it was always by a single goal. It was as if we'd forgotten how to create plays, which, for a hockey player, is like losing the joy of life. We could succeed only by making the other team fail, pulling them into the swamp. Our parents, at first confused, became irritated, then angry. Losing was bad enough, but losing like this turned the games into a slog. All the style and fun had gone out of it. Nor could they help noticing that, while some of our team's flashiest players—Duffy, Leo, Patrick—spent most of their time watching from the bench, Brian and Jenny never seemed to get off the ice. I noticed increased phone usage in the bleachers. At first I thought it was bored parents checking email, but when I got close, I saw that these people had in fact opened their Stopwatch apps and were timing the shifts, figuring out just how badly their kid was getting screwed. This can't be determined by the naked eye. It follows the Heisenberg Uncertainty Principle: your presence makes it impossible to take an accurate measurement. Or maybe it's more like Einstein's theory of relativity: whereas your child's minute on the ice flies, sixty seconds of Broadway Jenny feels endless.

———

> From Rich Cohen to Jerry Sherman, January 8, 9:33 p.m.:
>
> RC: It's fascinating to watch two people impose their will on an entire team.
>
> JS. Yup. Sour atmosphere. They're playing a different, tighter, more conservative game than before Christmas. It's a bit like watching adult hockey. They need to play hard for 1 minute then get off. No 3-minute shifts for anyone. They need to pass the puck and do it as hard as they shoot. And skate fast! They need to keep their sticks on the ice.

A player shouldn't spend more than a minute or so on the ice at a stretch—that's a shift. Beyond that, he slows and loses effectiveness. Hockey is a game of sprints. As a game intensifies—in the third period, say—the shifts should be shorter still. In the NHL playoffs, a skater might exit after twenty-five seconds of all-out effort. Most youth hockey teams run three forward lines. (In the pros, where games are longer and faster and more intense, they run four.) For every minute on, you get two minutes off—that is, two minutes of rest. With Brian and Jenny, the equation had been reversed. For every minute on the bench, they had two minutes on the ice. It was not hard for a parent to calculate the cold truth: though they were paying the same money and spending the same amount of time, Brian and Broadway Jenny were getting fifteen more minutes of ice time per game. And we were losing! Trapped in a spiral, which explained the mood on the Ridge-field side of the bleachers. (The benches were cold and so were our hearts.) It seemed stupid as well as unfair. But if you complained to Coach Hendrix, he'd blame your kid, saying, "Have you considered private skating lessons?" If you complained to

Coach Rizzo, he'd say, "Look, we want to get all the kids into a game, but we also want to win." If you called Coach Pete, you'd get his machine.

I pulled Coach Hendrix aside after a 5–0 loss to New Canaan.

I told him that what he was doing was wrong.

"What am I doing?"

"Jenny should not be getting triple Duffy's ice time."

"This lineup is our best chance to make it to the state tournament," he said. "Once we get there, if we get there, it's going to be because we played good team hockey."

"Why not let Duffy center the third line?"

"Jenny gives us a better chance."

"You can't accurately appraise your own kid," I said. "No one can."

"What are you saying?"

"I'm saying we need to get production from the entire team to win."

"Jenny gives us the best shot moving forward," he said coldly. "She's the better player."

"You know who else thought his kid represented the best shot moving forward?"

"Who?"

"Saddam Hussein."

Flu season lingered. At each practice, another player was missing, another family had succumbed. My wife got it, then I got it, then we all got it. Micah refused to drink Tamiflu. It was the taste. He said he'd rather have the flu than drink the medicine. We tried to disguise it in juice and in a milkshake, but he sniffed it out. I finally said, "Enough! Drink it!"

"If you make me drink it," he said, "I will vomit on the kitchen table."

I made him drink it, and he vomited on the kitchen table.

After a week, he said he felt strong enough to get back on skates.

I talked to Coach Hendrix before practice.

"Micah is still not a hundred percent," I said. "Please take it easy on him."

I usually skipped practices—they do not make good viewing—but I stuck around this time in case Micah needed me. It was depressing, not just the joyless drills but the overall mood. The kids worked without pucks. They just skated. Inside edge, outside edge. Down and back. Not only did Coach Hendrix *not* take it easy on Micah, but he seemed to push him harder than he did the others, as if sensing weakness. He had him skate extra laps for "dragging," made him sprint, made him do push-ups at center ice as the other kids counted, like something from a prison movie. I could see Micah's face through his mask. He looked bad. He fell near the end of a drill. Coach Hendrix stood over him, shouting, "Would you go down like that in a game?"

I banged on the glass to get Coach Hendrix's attention. He looked up myopically, as if he could neither see nor understand me. I signaled Micah, calling him off the ice. He ignored me. It was a *Cool Hand Luke* moment. He was not going to let Coach Hendrix break him.

Micah stumbled over after practice. His helmet was off, his face was flushed, and he was soaked with sweat. He looked wan in the dim rink light. He looked like one of those El Greco saints who, having died and been buried, suddenly stands up in the grave, clumps of earth falling from his hair. Once again, I asked myself, "What am I doing?" I remember Micah in his sonogram photo. He looked exactly the same.

I apologized to him. "I messed up," I said. "You shouldn't have been out there today. Get changed and we'll go home. And drink water. Drink as much water as you can stand."

Coach Hendrix had switched from sweats and skates to Dockers and Keds. I stopped him before he made it through the doors.

I said, "We need to talk."

We stood beside the Plexiglas that enclosed the rink. It was Thursday afternoon. The Bantams had taken the ice and were warming up for a game. The lobby was filled with kids and parents.

"What's up?"

"I told you that Micah's been sick. I asked you to take it easy on him. It seemed like you went after him even harder than normal. It's like you were trying to kill him out there."

"If he can't take it, he shouldn't be at practice," said Coach Hendrix. "It's one-size-fits-all. I don't treat anyone different than anyone else."

Looking into his eyes, I suddenly realized that Coach Hendrix hated me. It was in his look but also in his tone and between his words. At some point, I must have done or said something, and now he hated me, which meant he hated Micah.

"Some parents just can't stand it when someone coaches their kid," he said.

"What are you talking about?"

"You think your kid is perfect and no one is allowed to say a goddamn thing or precious sonny boy's feelings will get hurt."

"He had the flu."

"It's not the flu. It's him."

"What's your problem?"

"Your kid's my problem. I tell him what to do and he doesn't do it. Is he stupid, or what? He's always out of position. How can we play good team hockey when one of our wings is always out of position?"

"Tell me what you want him to do," I said, "and I will make sure he does it."

Coach Hendrix grunted, said, "Fine," got out a rub-off marker and drew on the Plexiglas. It was more of the same: dots and dashes, lines going every which way. I could make no sense of it. Then I suddenly understood and said, "You didn't play hockey growing up."

It was like an epiphany. It made sense of everything. No one who'd played the game as a kid would diagram a play this way. It was the sort of drawing done by a person who'd watched a lot of hockey on ESPN. Some of the other odd things Coach Hendrix had said made sense now, too. Like when he told Barry to never slow down in the neutral zone, because "once you slow down, it's hard to get going." That makes no sense to a twelve-year-old, but a lot of sense to a fiftysomething man who's just taken up adult hockey. Or the time he argued against scheduling two games in one day, because "it's just too damn hard on the body."

I must have touched a sensitive spot, because he went wild when I said that.

"So what if I didn't play?" he shouted. "You think you're

better than me because you played when you were a kid? I'm the one giving my time! I'm the one out there with the kids! I'm the one doing the schedule and scouting the competition and figuring out the algorithm! What are you doing? Nothing! Sitting on your ass in the stands bitching, like every other know-nothing hockey parent! I've spent hours! I was certified by USA Hockey. Were you certified? I sat through seminars. Did you sit through seminars? I learned about good team hockey. Did you learn about good team hockey? And now what? You want me to quit? Fine. I'll quit! I'll walk away right now."

The lobby had gotten quiet. People were staring.

I spoke in a whisper: "That's not what I meant."

I'd been caught off guard by his anger.

"I'd rather have a coach who never played but can teach than an NHL All-Star who can't talk to kids," I said. "It's just that, watching you draw that play, I realized you hadn't played when you were a kid, and it explains a lot. You can't remember what it was like to be eleven years old out there. A grown-up draws a bunch of arrows and lines, and your head swims, so you just skate away."

He stared at me.

"Don't you see what's happening?" I went on. "You draw these plays for the kids. They don't understand them but are afraid to tell you. So they pretend to understand and do their best, but it's wrong, and you get mad because you think they're not listening. They are listening. They just don't get it. I don't get it," I said, pointing at the play, which was already fading, "and I've been involved with hockey my entire life.

"Maybe you should encourage them a little more," I added. "You know, 'You get more flies with honey . . .'"

"I knew it!" he shouted. "You want me to kiss Micah's ass! Tell him he's great and give him a participation trophy."

"No," I said. "I just think it would be good to encourage as well as criticize. Maybe, for every three negative things, you can say one positive."

"What if there's nothing positive to say?"

"Make something up," I said. "Tell 'em you're glad they showed up on time."

"I won't do that," he said.

"Why not?"

"Because I'm not a hugger."

"Here's the problem," I said, getting angry myself. "Micah thinks you don't want him on this team. It's hard to work five days a week for a coach you think doesn't want you."

"He's right," said Coach Hendrix. "I don't want him."

"Try to hide it," I said.

"You think he's good, don't you?"

"I think he's one of our best players."

"Well, he's not," said Coach Hendrix. "He's not fast enough."

"He's faster than Jenny."

"He's not half as fast as Jenny."

"Let them race," I said. "Before the next practice, let them race. I'll bet you a thousand dollars Micah wins."

At this point, Coach Hendrix lost what remained of his self-control. He turned red and started waving his arms and shouting. He poured all his anger and disappointment on me—the fact that he'd not been able to play hockey as a kid, the fact that his older daughter had quit and his younger daughter had not made Double A, the fact that Jenny was now being swamped by kids like Micah and Duffy, the fact that he knew she'd quit, if not next year, then soon, and what was he supposed to do then? At that moment, I glimpsed the emptiness that awaits every hockey-loving hockey parent.

I shouted back, but can't remember what I said. I do remember wanting to punch him more than I have wanted to punch anyone since high school. I thought of how satisfying it would be. And he knew what I was thinking. I could see it in his eyes. Barry's mom, Gail, stepped between us and said, "Guys, you can't do this here."

He stormed out. I went to the bleachers and watched the Bantams play. This was a low point for me. I hated how I was acting but couldn't stop myself.

Micah was moved to the third line before the next game. Payback. Whenever a kid had to sit—because there was a two-and-ten penalty, say—it was Micah. He was in the penalty box literally and metaphorically, all because of me. Coach Hendrix took the occasion of Micah's demotion to reshuffle the lines yet again, freezing out all the kids he considered "uncoachable." These tended to be rambunctious boys. If they got serious ice time, it meant the game was already lost.

By the end of January, we'd just about played ourselves out of the state tournament. At Christmas, we'd been 19–11 and seemed to be a lock for the postseason. A month later, we were 19–20 and on the edge of elimination. It was not just the defeats. It was the scores of those defeats. We'd lost several games by more than five goals, which was death by algorithm. The parents talked about it constantly: how far we'd fallen, how much we'd have to win to get back into the race.

On January 29, we were five spots out of the state tournament. We played the Danbury Westerners at the Danbury Ice Arena on Independence Way. The Ice Arena is the most storied youth rink in Connecticut. It's our Boston Garden. This has to do with history. The rink, a boxy building in the center of town, was once home of the Danbury Trashers of the Federal Hockey League. The Trashers, who played at the lowest level of pro hockey—players made a few hundred bucks a game—had been acquired by a Genovese crime-family associate named Jimmy Galante. Galante worked in waste management, hence "Trashers." He bought the club for his son AJ's seventeenth birthday. As general manager, AJ negotiated deals by cell phone from his high school hallway, amassing the roster of skill players and goons that won Danbury's heart. To skirt the league's salary cap, Jimmy put the best players on the payroll of his company, Automated Waste Disposal Inc., where some made six figures as advisers or consultants. He then rebuilt the Ice Arena, which had been a neighborhood rink, into a first-rate facility, with banked seating, a high-tech scoreboard, concession stands, and plush locker rooms. The bleachers behind the home bench—Section 102—became the hangout of drunken bloodthirsty superfans, many of whom can still be identified by their Trasher tattoos. The team played two seasons before the Feds swooped in, arrested everyone, seized everything, and sent Jimmy Galante to prison.

I think of those delirious games whenever I step inside the Ice Arena. Jon "Nasty" Mirasty, the most feared fighter in the Federal League, battling at center ice. Brad "the Wingnut" Wingfield howling as his tibia, fibia, and ankle snapped, swearing revenge, which he took the next season. Wayne Gretzky's kid brother Brent—he scored thirteen goals for Danbury— leading the rush. Mobsters, having driven from New York, crowded into Jimmy's box. FBI agents gobbled frosty malts as they watched games and gathered evidence. Even the kids know something meaningful had happened here. This rink had once been an important place in the violent nether regions of pro hockey. If Madison Square Garden is Broadway, the Danbury Ice Arena is a roadhouse out on Highway 61. It's where hockey was worshipped by those who love it most. Anyone would want to be Mark Messier. You have to truly love this game to live like Nasty Mirasty.

The Bears changed, then stood along the Plexiglas. They should have been tense. We needed to win this game, but they seemed happy. All that losing had lowered expectations, setting them free. They goofed around in warm-ups, ignoring Coach Hendrix's demands to "knock it off." The game started. Micah played left wing on the third line. He played well when he got in the game, which was not often. He'd skate twenty or thirty seconds, then Coach Hendrix would wave him off. It was as if every time he saw Micah he remembered our fight and became enraged. He actually yanked Micah from a two-on-one, a good scoring chance. Micah smashed his stick in frustration. This bugged me—a good stick can cost two hundred bucks. The teams were so well matched it felt as if they were playing before a mirror. In fact, many of the Danbury kids lived in Ridgefield—they were youth hockey refugees, having fled the complications of our program. This gave the contest an internecine feel.

When everything else is equal, look for the incongruity— that'll be the difference. On that day, it was a Danbury defenseman named Ilya Gogol. He stood six-foot-three in skates, a giant among boys, a shark among minnows. We'd heard about him all year. He was a legend. Tall, fast, and remorseless, a big kid with soft hands. We heard he was a foreign-exchange student, a Russian visitor living with the Danbury coach and his family. They called it educational, but we knew a ringer when we saw one. If he wasn't dominating a game, it was only because he wasn't in the mood. That's how it seemed anyway, for now and then, and with great ease, he'd pick up the puck, skate through our entire team, and beat Arcus with a flick of the wrist. Gogol had a great slap shot, too. He could hit the post at fifty feet, like a hunter picking a bird off a wire. If shot wide, the puck whipped around the boards like an ivorine ball circling a roulette wheel. He was a nearly impossible obstacle for our forwards. No one could get around the Russian. He blasted anyone who got close to his goalie. I'm not sure why he didn't just take over the game and win it by himself. Maybe he considered it unsporting. Maybe he didn't want to draw the wrong kind of attention. Maybe he was easily bored. In any case, the score was even at the end of the first period.

At times like this, I wonder if the lack of hitting—checking is not legal in Pee Wee—puts the smaller kids at a long-term disadvantage. Checking at an early age teaches things no coach ever can—not just about hitting but about how to avoid getting hit, how to be crafty and skirt the blows, how to use a big kid's size against him. It teaches you to keep your head up and your eyes on the distance. It teaches you to monitor every player, never losing track of the player who can hurt you, to always know exactly where on the ice that person is. Had I been playing against Danbury, I would have charted Gogol's every move as a matter of survival. But today's players learn the game in a hockey fantasyland without predators, so skate obliviously, head down, in and out of the fumes of semitrucks. The Russian—the eighteen-wheeler of the previous metaphor—was not *trying* to hit anyone. He was just going where he was going. What was he supposed to do if you got in his way?

He'd only recently come into this big body and hardly knew how to operate the thing himself.

Patrick Campi was having the game of his life. If the score was close—we were tied at two halfway through the second—credit Patrick. He'd led the rush from the right wing, backchecked with energy, passed and shot in a way that took him all over the ice. He set up the first goal, skirting the defense by flicking the puck to himself off the boards, then finding Barry with a long pass that put him one-on-one with the goalie. He scored the second himself, a wrist shot that found its way through Danbury's defense. And yet, all the while, Patrick was moving closer to the Russian, closer and closer, dangerously close. It was like watching a loved one dance on the edge of a cliff. My heart was in my mouth. Patrick had a history of concussions. His mother told us that one more might end his hockey career.

With less than two minutes left in the second, Patrick passed the puck to Tommy McDermott, who passed it back. Danbury's left wing grazed the puck as it went by, disturbing but not intercepting it. Patrick turned and reached for the puck and, as he did, took his eyes off the ice. The Russian, going for the same puck, skated right through as if Patrick were not even there. The collision, which hardly slowed the Russian, demolished Patrick. He was flung, losing his mouth guard, stick, and gloves. He lay sprawled, as if shot, at center ice. His eyes were closed, his face expressionless and pale. People said Patrick had been "laid out," but the term does not do the event justice. It was more like he'd been crumpled. The rink got eerily quiet, the kind of quiet only a crowd can make.

We'd all seen something scary, and the mood that formed around the scary thing was somber and somehow sacred.

From there, we got the usual protocol, the procession that follows every youth hockey injury: first comes the collision; then the ref blows his whistle, skates over, looks down and talks, or tries to talk, to the kid; then the ref waves to the bench; meanwhile, the other players have taken a knee. It's a kind of group prayer that suggests the gravity of the moment and the brevity of life. We urge the wayward hockey soul, which is circling the scoreboard, to reenter the body so the game can resume. An assistant or parent coach walks across the ice—Coach Hendrix, hands buried in the pockets of his Bears windbreaker. If the injury seems serious, as it did with Patrick, the assistant or parent waves over a second assistant or parent-coach—Coach Rizzo in Timberlands. At this point, the injured kid will almost always sit up, get to his feet, then skate warily back to the bench as the parents clap. But Patrick stayed down. He was down for what felt like hours. Paramedics were called. He was helped off the ice and taken to a nearby hospital. He'd suffered a moderate concussion, which, compounded by fear—the weirdness of the situation, all those people looking down—would keep him off the ice for at least a month.

The Pee Wee A Bears and their parents were rattled by the injury. We could not get the image of Patrick down at center ice out of our minds, nor could we stop thinking about worst-case scenarios. Ilya Gogol, the Russian, sat at the end of the Danbury bench with his helmet off. He stared into space, shaken. Even worse than getting hurt is hurting someone else. For the best of us, one goal of life is to get through it doing as little damage as possible. He came back for the third period—he'd not even committed a penalty; the contact was incidental—but had been neutralized by remorse.

Leo Moriarty took Patrick's place on the second line. Leo had been underused, supposedly because he missed so many practices for lacrosse. But lacrosse season had been over for a month and they were still not playing Leo, though he usually made something happen on the ice. I knew why Coach Hendrix hated Micah, or thought I did. Because he hated me. But why did he hate Leo? "That's easy," said Jerry Sherman. "Because he wears flip-flops to the rink."

Broadway Jenny won the first face-off after the injury. She played the puck to Leo, who sped up ice, faking this way and that, splitting the defense, "like Moses splitting the Red Sea," said Leo's father, Albert, happily. Leo slowed as he approached the Danbury goalie, waited, waited . . . then shot. You always have more time than you think. Most coaches want you to get the puck off your stick as fast as possible, but in truth, shooting late can be just as effective as shooting early.

We won the game less with a cry of victory than a sigh of relief.

FEBRUARY

I can't be alone in hating February more than other months. It's cold and dark. You might get a few hints of spring—a warm wind, a robin blown off course—but it's mostly a never-ending tundra of pain. Some days are bitter, others more bitter still. On subzero mornings, you dress like a polar explorer just to reach the car. When you spit, it freezes in the air and slides like a Pee Wee skater along the frozen crust of the earth. "I know how the Okies felt," I told my wife. "I just want to load the jalopy and head for California."

If February 2019 is remembered at all, it's for what I consider the oddest game of the season. When people ask about the absurdities of youth hockey, it's this game I tell them about. We were playing the Wild Haven Wombats at the Winter Garden. As Jerry Sherman says, "Beware the Havens." Micah told me it was a kind of all-star team, the sort that is not supposed to exist. There'd been no tryouts. The coach, a burly man with a red beard, had instead gone from rink to rink at the end of the previous season, watching games and recruiting kids. He'd approach them in the parking lot in the way of a meth dealer: "Hey, pal, wanna play for a winner?" He'd offered cost breaks and incentives—this team was not meant to earn but to be a kind of showpiece, an advertisement for the rest of the program. The result was a mix of excellent skaters and goons. They played fast and clean when possible, slow and dirty when necessary. Their club motto was printed on their equipment bags: "If we can't beat you, we can at least beat you up."

Coach Hendrix had been warned but scheduled the game anyway.

"The algorithm," he explained. "If we play them tight, we'll jump five spots."

Coach Hendrix gave the Bears a pregame rundown of several Wild Haven standouts. He told them to watch out for a kid named Clay Lowdermilk, who was tall, blue-eyed, and long-haired. He'd been suspended for fighting in September and suspended again in October.

"He can hurt you," said Coach Hendrix.

He named several other Wild Haven players, including a pair of fast, high-scoring twins whom their hockey-loving parents had named "Messier" and "Graves."

"Their sister is named Madison after Madison Square Garden," Coach Hendrix added, "but don't worry about her. She doesn't play."

The teams stared at each other during the warm-up. Judd Meese told me Wild Haven had lost only one game all year. Parky said, "They look like a bunch of jerks."

The Wombats did have an arrogant swagger. That's what tailored recruitment and a fearsome reputation will do. They gathered together before the face-off and put their hands in a circle. Clay Lowdermilk led the cheer: "Two, four, six, eight, let's go annihilate. Wombats!"

In a game like this, if the refs lose control early, it'll never be regained. That's what happened. Wild Haven came after our kids less like a team of Pee Wees than like the Jets in *West Side Story*, all elbows and slew foots and cross-checks. When they scored, it seemed less the intended outcome and more a side effect of the real mission, which was to humiliate the Bears. At one point, late in the first period, five of our kids were down on the ice at the same time. The Winter Garden looked like the scene of a bizarre mob hit.

Micah limped off the ice at the end of one shift. Later, when I asked what had happened, he said, "I got credit-carded."

"'Credit-carded'? What does that even mean?"

"A kid's skate blade went up my butt."

Coach Hendrix called a time-out. Several of the Wombats had taken multiple penalties. "Let's use that," said Coach Hendrix, reminding the kids of the automatic ejection that awaits any player with more than four penalties. "If they keep going like this, half their team will be gone before the third." He picked out a handful of forwards—Duffy and Tommy, Micah and Joey—and told them to trash-talk the gooniest Wild Haven players. "Chirp at them," he said, "especially Lowdermilk. Goad them into taking penalties, then, with the goons gone, we can get to work."

Tommy and Joey were on the ice at the start of the second period. Joey crashed into Lowdermilk. The height difference meant that Joey's head, or more specifically, his helmet, hit Clay Lowdermilk in the ribs. The blow sent both kids reeling. Joey said something—chirping, as ordered—as Lowdermilk skated away. Lowdermilk stopped and skated back, looming over Joey. Words were exchanged. Lowdermilk punched Joey in the head. Joey stood there stunned as Lowdermilk landed three more blows. Joey charged Lowdermilk, throwing hay-makers as they both fell. Tommy, seeing his stepbrother in trouble, dove on Lowdermilk, too.

Parents from both sides were banging on the glass, scream-ing at the referees, who pulled the kids apart.

"No penalty box for these three," the ref told the score-keeper (Terry Stanley). "They're ejected. Goodbye. Gone."

Micah exiting stage left

Coach Hendrix told Micah and Roman Holian to serve the time in the box. We were losing 5–1 at that point. Three of their players soon collected a fifth penalty and were like-wise ejected. We lost Rick Stanley for taking five. Rick, our big, left-handed defenseman, moved about as well as a traffic cone but played with an anger that could be helpful in a game like this. His father was, as I've said, a serious Deadhead. It was like San Francisco '69 in his truck. Rick had formed his personality in opposition. That's the edge you saw in the Wild

Haven game. On the score sheet, it read as "hooking, inter-ference, cross-checking, checking, roughing." On the ice, it was beautiful rage.

Duffy Taylor, normally our biggest hothead, had been sur-prisingly calm all game, perhaps because he was so locked in. He scored in the first period, then again in the second. He rode the stick as if it were a pony after that second goal. But he looked exhausted on the bench. All the ejections meant a shortage of personnel. Duffy was skating far more than he was used to.

"I took him to lunch at Friday's before the game," said Parky. "I hope that wasn't a mistake."

The score was 5–3 going into the third. Duffy drank some water, grabbed his stick, and went out. He won the face-off, then was on the rush with Leo and Roman. Leo came up the left side. Duffy skated behind him. Leo dropped the puck to Duffy, who blasted a shot through a defender's legs. It hit the crossbar and bounced up into the netting. The whistle blew. Duffy turned to skate to the bench, slowed, bent over, and puked. He never stopped skating, so the puke became a long, chocolate-colored trail on the ice.

The referee either did not notice the puke or was pretend-ing not to. He carried the puck to the circle for a face-off. Jack Camus had come out in Duffy's place. Parents from both teams were screaming at the ref.

"Hey, ref," Leo's father, Albert, shouted. "There's puke on the ice."

The ref skated over and examined the puke, looked up at Albert, and said, "What do you want me to do about it?"

"I don't know," said Albert. "Something."

"I'm only paid to officiate," said the ref, returning to the circle.

Coach Rizzo went out and squirted some water on the puke. Everyone seemed to agree that that was good enough. And still, the puke remained, a Bermuda Triangle to be avoided at all costs.

Micah was skating without the puck in our own zone a few shifts later. He was poke-checking a kid from Wild Haven when another kid stepped in front and blocked him, which is not allowed. It's interference. Micah, sent sprawling, jumped to his feet and slashed the kid who'd hit him, and *that's* what the ref saw, and *that's* the only penalty he called. Micah's third: roughing, cross-checking, slashing. I could see him stewing in the box. As soon as he'd served his time, he went back on the ice, found and tackled the kid who'd hit him. What's worse, they both landed in the puke. The Wild Haven parents booed. One of them said, "What is this, pro wrestling? Why doesn't he just climb up onto the ropes!"

I could hear Coach Hendrix screaming at Micah, calling him stupid and selfish. That was Micah's fourth penalty, but its flagrance made it count as two. He was ejected. Roman had to sit Micah's double minor.

Later in the third, when Wild Haven had opened up a 9–4 lead, Broadway Jenny was called for hooking.

Coach Hendrix screamed at the ref: "That was no fucking penalty! You need glasses! You're blind. I bet your parents are blind, too. And your kids."

The ref gave Coach Hendrix a two-minute minor for heckling, which, once again, was served by Roman.

Broadway Jenny was in the box when the game ended, feet out, head back, singing "Naughty," a song from the show *Matilda*. Her voice, plaintive and high, could be heard all over the rink: "Just because you find that life's not fair it / Doesn't mean that you just have to grin and bear it."

The Bears were quiet in the locker room after the game. There'd been a total of forty penalty minutes, a franchise record. Four of our players—Joey, Tommy, Micah, Rick—had been ejected and would have to sit out the next game, too. Coach Hendrix was suspended for two games. Another such showing, and the Pee Wee A Bears would be disqualified from the state tournament, a fate that had befallen only one other local club, the Long Island Cruisers, banned for putting excrement—possibly canine, possibly human—in a visiting team's equipment bags.

Coach Hendrix made each of our ejected players stand up and give a postgame analysis.

"Tell us why we lost," he said.

After the kids had spoken, Coach Hendrix turned on them, pointed, and said, "Wrong! It's you! You four are the reason we lost! If you hadn't lost control and been ejected, we could have won that game."

Micah and I watched the Zamboni prepare the rink for the next game. The puke was still there, only it was being covered with a fresh coat of ice. This had to stand for something, though neither one of us could figure out what.

The Wild Haven game and its ejections turned out to be my breaking point. The weather, the losing, the parent-coaches, penalties, and recriminations—it was too much. My heart started racing. Beads of sweat appeared on my forehead.

I couldn't stop the stream of nonsense flowing through my mind. I went to the doctor, who sent me to a cardiologist, who gave me tests, charged me several thousand dollars, then sent me home with instructions to "calm down." I blamed hockey, not the game but the culture, ins and outs, favorites and outcasts. According to my father, "The secret to life is caring, but not that much."

I was having trouble following his advice.

My wife decided I should take a break from youth hockey.

"It's not that it will kill you," she said, "but that it'd be such a stupid reason to die."

"So what should I do?" I asked.

"Take some time off," she said. "I'll deal with the practices and games. It'll be here when you get back."

I knew she was right. I needed a break from the game as much as I've ever needed anything. If I did not get away from these parents and these kids, from these rinks and punishments and coaches and lectures and losses, I'd fall down and foam at the mouth.

"But Micah . . ."

"Micah will be fine."

And so Jessica and I swapped jobs. She drove Micah to hockey. I drove Aaron and Nate to mock trial and theater, noble pursuits that I cared about, but not that much. I took up daily meditation. I'd sit in the car outside the playhouse, focus on my breathing, clear my mind and think about nothing. Jessica updated me on the games and the team, though I sensed she was not telling me everything.

Jerry Sherman filled in the gaps, sending texts that grew in detail the longer I stayed away:

February 16, 9:33 p.m.:

JS: 12 penalties! And we . . . tie. Apparently this team is ranked higher, so it's like a win. Kids played better. Great game. We should have won, but typical of our coaching staff we had a line in for 2+ minutes and New Canaan had fresh legs. Dan had at least 50 saves. We are a morning team. Micah played well. I think we do ourselves a disservice by not changing the lines. Barry doesn't pass, and Rick and Brian's chances of going to Ivy League institutions are in jeopardy.

February 17, 1:15 p.m.:

JS: Micah just scored! 3–1.

February 23, 1:19 p.m.:

JS: Micah just got another one! 4–2

JS: Just finished. Great game. Other team had about 10 penalties. 4–3. Other team was better. Very lucky.

February 24, 10:11 a.m.:

JS: What a nightmare . . . kids for the other team were yelling at refs and once again I noticed gun stickers on the other team's cars. Rough crowd. But two win weekends are good.

RC: Were they also from Gun Haven?

JS: I told them I wanted to run a urine check on their kids. Newington and surrounding areas. Troubled youth.

February 25, 4:03 p.m.:

RC: How'd the game go?

JS: We lost 1–0.

JS: Micah had best game. Goalie too.

JS: I don't understand the sport.

JS: Rizzo tells me Barry was having an off game. Barry always looks the same to me. He doesn't pass.

RC: I think that kid needs glasses.

JS: Honest?

RC: Honest.

JS: I don't like it when Hendrix's kid plays so much. It feels dirty.

JS: Brian and Rick have moments when they forget they are not supposed to let people skate right past them.

JS: The talk was our team was sleeping. If that's the case, they are the best-rested team in Connecticut.

February 27, 9:04 p.m.:

RC: Just heard that if we make it to Tier 3 states we might play the Ridgefield Double As. Think we have a shot? It'd take a miracle just to get there. We should show them the old Rocky movie. Ya know, "Nobody's ever gone the distance with Creed."

JS: Playing the Double As? I hadn't heard that. Who told you?

RC: Micah. Said he heard it from Coach Rizzo.

JS: That'd be great, but we have a lot of work to do before that. Been watching our defense close, and they really make a shitload of mistakes. Rick and Brian are loose. Team today exposed them badly.

Duffy is a hothead, a penalty waiting to happen.
Tommy is going good. Micah is lights-out. Roman,
Leo, and my Broadway Julie are starting to see some
fog on the mirror.

JS: Forgot to mention. Micah was down twice. One kid
tackled him. I didn't see the other hit. He was OK but
he got up slow. I think he just lost his wind. I dropped
an eff bomb when he got tackled. The five away dads
were looking at the floor.

JS: Miss ya :)

It was a team parent confab that brought me back. We met at the Hideaway, a local bar where we talked and drank and crunched the numbers in search of an answer to the ultimate question: Just what did the kids need to do to make it to the postseason? Our record was 32–28 on Valentine's Day. According to the algorithm, we'd need forty wins to reach Tier 2 of the Connecticut state tournament. We had fourteen games left to play. Three of these were against teams we had no realistic chance of beating. Three were against teams we should roll over. Eight could go either way. We'd need to run up the score in the easy games, hang tight in the impossible ones, and win at least five of the toss-ups. We took the kids aside before the next practice and laid it all out. Instead of saying, "You must do this," we asked them, "Do you want to make it to the state tournament? Because here is what it will take."

Why do we push our kids? Why do we put them in high-pressure situations? Why do we treat them in a way that we ourselves would resent being treated? No one knows what sort of engine drives the sports parent. A friend is always there to absolve you, to say, "You just want what's best for your kid." It sounds right. It lets you off the hook. But then, as you watch the Zamboni, you ask yourself, "Is that true? Is that why I behave this way? Because I want what's best for my kid?" The answer is yes and no. Yes, that is what you want, but that's not all that you want. It'd be nice for him to win, but it'd also be nice for *you* to watch him win, nice to talk about and remember. It'd make you feel good about him and also good about yourself. You'd believe you'd done something right. You want what's best for your kid, but who even knows what that is? Maybe it's succeeding at hockey, but maybe it's failing. Maybe it's quitting altogether. Maybe it's winning, but maybe it's losing. Being a good person is hard.

Coach Pete returned a few days after we'd explained the task to the team (how many games they needed to win, etc.). He did not say where he'd been, or what he'd been doing, or if he was back for good, but something about him was different. He'd changed in the way Mike Ditka had changed after his heart attack. Chicago Bears fans will know what I'm talking about: the coach, with his mustache and sweater vests and polyester pants, had been a kind of communal gym teacher for the kids of Chicagoland, calling us shirkers and making us drop and give him twenty "good ones." He looked the same when he got out of the hospital, but different, too. He seemed smaller, wiser. He'd had a brush with the infinite. He knew something he had not known before. He'd looked back on his career and had seen dark places where the love and fun should have been. He wanted to continue living the same life but experience it in a different way. He'd gained perspective, realized, in the way only a brush with death can teach, that all this is real. Something like this happened to Coach Pete. For the first time all season, the practices became fun. Coach Pete tore up Coach Hendrix's game plan and simply let the kids play. He turned everything into a contest. He took the team out for pizza. Instead of grueling off-ice training—stretches and knee bends—he had them play dodgeball and led them on hikes through the woods.

Coach Rizzo seemed OK with it, but Coach Hendrix was pissed.

"If you wanted to do this kind of thing at the start of the season, fine," he told Coach Pete, "but not now, when every game is do-or-die."

Coach Pete pointed at the kids up the trail and said, "By climbing hills, they're working the same muscles they'd be working in dryland training."

He shuffled the lines, moving Joey McDermott, who'd been playing defense, to wing, where he'd skate beside his stepbrother Tommy, because, as Coach Pete said, "brothers don't need words to communicate." This adjustment alone led to an offensive burst. He moved Micah, too. When playing left wing, Micah has a tendency to cherry-pick. He camps at the blue line, waiting for the puck and a breakaway. It dulls him—while waiting, his feet and mind slow. He's better at center, where he's forced to play at both ends of the ice. So that's where Coach Pete put him, third-line center, with Broadway Jenny on one wing and Barry Meese—whose father, at my insistence, had taken Barry to the optometrist; he was now wearing corrective lenses, and it made all the difference—on the other. Patrick Campi, back from his concussion, centered the top line. Duffy Taylor played second-line center. What followed was a return of the wide-open style that characterized the first weeks of the season. It was like the recurrence of a favorite childhood melody, a song from better times. Coach Pete used this style—the breakouts, the three-on-twos—to build plays, which we worked on in practice. In other words, he did not try to teach the kids new skills so that they could execute plays downloaded from the internet, but rather designed plays around what they were doing already.

In this way, the team came to grapple with a basic hockey conundrum: How does a decent team beat a good or even a very good team? How can the mediocre be made to defeat the excellent?

Passing is a big part of the answer. You can beat speed by spreading out and moving the puck, using the entire ice. No player is faster than a strong pass. Hustle is another part. When hockey coaches want to remind players to hustle, they tell them to keep moving their feet, which is confusing. Here's what they mean: never stop going. Think about running: if you stop, you stop. A hockey player glides, which is what a lot of kids do when they get tired. Instead of telling the kids to "move their feet," Coach Pete told them to "keep pedaling," which they understood right away. He also reminded them to "make a move." "You hardly ever beat a goalie because you've got a great shot," he explained. "You beat a goalie with your brain. If you trick him and get him to move out of position, you'll be shooting into an empty net."

Persistence is another key, especially over the course of a season. It's a talent just like speed or good hands. It's what keeps a person working when everyone else has quit. Maybe it's obtuseness. Maybe players with that kind of talent are too dumb to know they've been licked. "When I played, I never sat on the bench," the Chicago Bears safety Doug Plank told me. "You know why? I wanted to watch Walter Payton. I would stand on that sideline and just look: the way he hustled, even in games when we were hopelessly behind, you could learn from that. If you put on a tape and watch a player and cannot tell from the way he plays whether his team is ahead or behind—that's who you want."

The Pee Wee As blazed through the second half of February, winning twice as much as they lost, even taking some of the games the parents had considered unwinnable. If this were a movie, and let's face it, everything is a movie, I'd show these halcyon days in a montage. There'd be shots of kids—Micah and Barry, Broadway Jenny and Broadway Julie, Brian, Dan, Tommy and Joey—entering arenas in khakis and ties, headphones on their ears, flashing the hang-loose sign, striding onto the ice in superslow-mo, like Apollo astronauts gliding along in space helmets and silver suits. There'd be close-ups and panoramas from each game: Brian Rizzo beating the Darien goalie with a slap shot, sliding on his knees in celebration; Barry flying on a breakaway; Tommy McDermott lacing a no-look pass to Joey McDermott, who finishes the play with a one-timer; Dan doing the split and the butterfly, making every kind of save, snagging a puck out of the air—all of it set to power ballads like, "Seven Nation Army," and "Dude Looks Like a Lady."

On the last day of the month, Coach Pete stuck his head in the locker room door to deliver the news: "Hey, guys. You made the state tournament." I will not describe the ensuing scene, but instead urge you to go on the internet and look up footage of the Chicago Cubs celebrating the playoff win that put the team in its first World Series in 108 years.

MARCH

Many years ago, John Belushi delivered a brilliant *SNL* commentary on the month of March. He was specifically interested in the ways that month swings like a door between winter and spring. Starting with the cliché "March comes in like a lion and goes out like a lamb," he went on to describe the various ways March "comes in" and "goes out" in different parts of the world, such as Norway, where, he insisted, it comes in like a polar bear and goes out like a walrus; and Honduras, where it comes in like a lamb and goes out like a salt marsh harvest mouse; and the Maldives, where it comes in like a wildebeest and goes out like an ant, "a tiny little ant"; and South Africa, where it comes in like a lion and goes out like a different lion—"one has a mane, and one doesn't have a mane"; and South America, where it "swims in like a sea otter and slithers out like a giant anaconda."

In Ridgefield in 2019, March came in like a lion and went out like the same lion. The month started and ended with a blizzard. We had rain, ice, hail, wind, frost, freeze, black ice, and flooding in the days between. The first storm consisted of pepperoni-size snowflakes that accumulated hour after hour on the narrow roads. They muffled every sound, cushioned every step. It was a cake crust, a wonderland. The dog disappeared in the snow. We saw her tail moving in the distance like a dorsal fin. We were captives in the house, waiting for plows. The drivers were giddy from lack of sleep when they finally arrived at 4:00 a.m. It was hard to tell those who'd made erratic patterns in the snow because they were exhausted from those who'd made erratic patterns in the snow because they were drunk. The second storm consisted of BB-size flakes that piled up fast. The trees were sheathed in ice at dawn, the roads slick as salesmen. Then the air warmed and the sun came out and the snow melted. The sound of cracking ice and rushing water was everywhere. The days got longer. In the morning, as you lay in bed, you'd listen to the birds at the feeder and think, "I'm going to make it."

The state tournament was played at Yale University's Ingalls Rink, in New Haven, at the end of March. A famous building, it was designed in the 1950s by Eero Saarinen. It's easy to see a relation between the rink and some of the architect's other iconic work—the Gateway Arch in Saint Louis, the TWA Flight Center at JFK International Airport—in the sloped roof and cathedral-like interior that give the facility its nickname, the Whale.

The tournament followed a two-round structure: each of twenty participating teams would play two games in the first round; the eight teams with the most first-round points would continue to a second round of single-elimination play that would culminate in the championship. Being the last seeds in the tournament, the Pee Wee A Bears were not expected to win a single game. We were cannon fodder, bums who'd overachieved just by making it to the Whale.

I spent the first day of the tournament wandering the lobby, writing down the names of each club, which I spotted on equipment bags and jackets. The Fairfield Rangers. The Greenwich Cardinals. The Hamden Green Dragons. The Salisbury Redhawks. The Shoreline Sharks. The Norwich Seahawks. The Southern Connecticut Storm. The Stamford Sharks. The Colebrook Galassis. The Wallingford Rockets. The West Hartford Wolves. The Bridgeport Wizards. The Yale Bulldogs. The New Canaan Winter Club. The Danbury Doves. The Griffin Flames. The Southern Stars.

The Pee Wee A Bears dumped their bags near the locker room and went out to watch the Ridgefield Double As play West Hartford. If I were a different sort of writer, I would end the story here, on a high, because it was a mission-accomplished moment—our kids had indeed caught the top team, the coach of which had rejected every one of them.

The Double As raced up and down the ice, led by the best Double A in the state, a big kid named George Matoose, who would soon ascend to Triple A, then continue on to prep school. Matoose had a way of making his teammates look better than they actually were; it was his passing, which pushed and pulled kids into position. The game stayed close through two periods, when West Hartford, which had been smothering on defense, made the mistake of chasing Matoose. This opened passing lanes and left players uncovered. Matoose found every open teammate. A cascade of goals followed.

The West Hartford Wolves had a Russian coach. You could tell by his intensity and by his accent, which could be heard all over the facility when he shouted, "Skate, you sons of bitches! Skate!"

Our kids were outside their locker room when the game ended (Ridgefield AA 7, West Hartford 2). The hall was filled with players and parents. West Hartford came through with their helmets off, red-faced, sweating. Some were crying, others crying hysterically. This was round one, game one. It made you think, "My God, what does that coach do to them?" Then I saw him. He was wearing a gold team jacket, his dark hair slicked back—Brylcreem? pomade?—like a memory of Leonid Brezhnev. His name was stitched on his breast pocket: Gabe Petrenko. His son—the kid had the same last name on his jersey—walked a few yards behind, head down, sniffling. Coach Petrenko muttered in Russian, turned and yelled in English: "You know what you are, Dmitri? Human fucking garbage." Dmitri followed his father into the locker room and slammed the door. Our players could hear Coach Petrenko yelling through the wall. I saw him in the lobby later. He was laughing on the phone, saying, "Yes, baby. I love you, too."

If I coached, my pregame talks would be stemwinders. I'd call on the kids to "give a hundred and ten percent" and "leave it all out on the ice." But contemporary youth coaches tend to shy away from grand pronouncements. I've yet to hear one of them speak the sentence that was standard in my day: "You are the best team I've ever coached." It's as if they are afraid of saying the wrong thing and getting hung by their own words. It's another thing we can blame on social media. Every one of the great pep talks of my childhood, riddled with words like "pussy" and "wimp," would get a coach fired today. Coach Pete was especially subdued before the first game. He spoke softly. I was standing outside the open locker room door and had to lean in to hear him. "It's been a long season, and you have worked hard," he said. "Here is your chance to shine. Here is your chance to prove you can play with anyone. Just remember, forwards, stay in your lanes. And defenseman, keep the puck away from Dan, even if that means stepping in front of a shot. Now . . . Bears on three!"

Parky and I had been tasked with keeping score, which meant sitting in a box near the team bench and recording every goal, assist, and penalty. We shuffled across the ice to assume our Plexiglas perch. You feel like Eichmann on trial out there, the man in the glass booth. We were playing the Bridgeport Wizards, a team that had already beaten us twice this season. They blew us out in the fall. We played them closer in the winter. That game had ended with Duffy Taylor swinging his stick like Joe Pesci in a mob movie. Our kids did not seem to remember any of that, though. They played like a new team at the start of a new season.

Micah scored on his first shift. The first goal of the game,

it came on a breakaway. He put the puck through a defense-man's legs. I was openly rooting, a violation of the score-keeper's code. I couldn't help it. (I used to identify with the quarterback leading the two-minute drill. My empathy now goes to the parents in the stands.) I could see the back of his jersey as he made his way toward the goalie, blades churning, ice flying. I could see the number 45 on his helmet and back. I could hear other Ridgefield parents screaming his name—the name that my wife and I carefully selected for him, the name meant to honor my grandfather Morris, who came to this country in steerage in 1910. My heart was in my mouth. I prayed to God: "Oh dear Lord, though it be trivial, please let my son have this goal." Something in me never believes he will finish the play. There will be cheering, but not for him. But he did finish it, using a move that works at every level, from Pee Wee to NHL: fake the forehand, shoot with the backhand. The referee skated to the scorers' table with the official line: "Number forty-five, unassisted, thirteen forty-five in the first." Parky slapped me on the back, saying, "Every time your kid scores, an angel gets its wings."

Tommy McDermott added another goal in the second. Brian Rizzo tacked on one more in the third. Dan Arcus stopped thirty-five shots. We won that first game with ease.

The Pee Wee A Bears played again the following night. There was a full moon over the Long Island Sound. The temperature had been climbing all week. The gears rumble, the seasons change. The Bears were outmuscled and outweighed by their game-two opponents, the Norwich Seahawks, junk-food-raised goons who pushed our kids all over the ice. One of the Seahawks, a defenseman with a wispy mustache named Delvecchio, looked less like a youth hockey player than like a TV detective, the sort that lives on a houseboat in the Intracoastal Waterway. Judd Meese nudged me as the kid skated by, saying, "Maybe he'll buy me a beer after the game."

The first period started with Delvecchio hip-checking Broadway Jenny into the boards, possibly to set a tone of general menace. Though splayed on the ice—gloves here, stick there, helmet askew—Broadway Jenny refused to stay down. Her toughness was amazing, her courage. She crawled around, feeling for her equipment, got to her skates, and sprinted back into the play. The crowd, even a few of the Norwich parents, were with us after that. They cheered whenever Broadway Jenny got the puck or stepped out of the face-off circle to reposition the wings. She stood for the resilience and determination of our team. We beat them because we refused to lose. Duffy was our star, passing and shooting, rushing opponents, forcing turnovers. He had his best assist of the season, a long pass that carried the puck from our goal line clear to center ice, where it found Broadway Jenny in full stride. You watched such plays with excitement and regret—this is what we could have been all along if they'd backed off and let the kids play. We won the game 6–4. Duffy got a hat trick. Parky sat proudly in the lobby as the kids changed, defiant and redeemed.

———

The call came late that night. It was Coach Rizzo. He could hardly contain his glee.

"We're playing the Double As!"

"When?"

"Tomorrow, five p.m."

It felt like vindication, even if it smelled like napalm. Our kids had been treated like dogs, and the dogs had caught the bus. It meant our kids, who had been judged unworthy for the Double A team, would finally have their chance.

The parents spent the rest of the night calling each other to revel. When I spoke to Patrick Campi's mom, Sue, she was near tears. Patrick was a second-year Pee Wee, a year older than Micah. He'd played on the same team as the current Double As the previous season, as had Tommy McDermott and Barry Meese. They were the only kids from that team not to make the cut. At Lake Placid, where all the Ridgefield kids mingle, the Double As refused to socialize with the Single As. It was a matter of hierarchy. "Patrick had been best friends with those kids just last year and they wouldn't even talk to him," said Sue. "Can you imagine?"

"No," I said.

"You know what?" she said. "I hope we kick their ass."

The players were usually supposed to arrive an hour before a game. Considering the special nature of this contest, we'd been told to have them at the Whale by 3:00 p.m., 120 minutes before face-off. It meant pulling our kids—sixth and seventh graders—out of school early. ("So much for teaching priorities," said my wife, writing the permission slip.)

"Why so early?" I asked.

"Coach Pete wants to say something," Coach Rizzo told me.

But when we got to the rink the next afternoon, Coach

Pete was not there. The kids played bubble hockey as they waited. The parents stood in the holy hockey circle, gossiping. When it was 3:40 and Coach Pete had still not arrived, the parents became restless. At 4:00 p.m., some started to panic.

Coach Hendrix went outside to call Coach Pete. He seemed confused when he came back. "I tried his cell, his office, and his house," he said. "He's not picking up."

"Maybe he's in traffic," said Judd Meese.

"What traffic?"

"Maybe he got a late start," said Sue Campi.

"Yeah, but why wouldn't he answer his cell?" asked Parky Taylor.

"Try his wife," said Coach Rizzo.

"I tried his wife," said Coach Hendrix.

"Try his brother," said Judd Meese.

"I tried his brother and his sister," said Coach Hendrix. "No answer."

At 4:15 p.m., Broadway Jenny and Brian led the team out to the parking lot for dryland warm-ups (jumps, stretches, etc.).

Coaches Rizzo and Hendrix huddled in a back hall, coming up with a plan. In the absence of Coach Pete, the parent-coaches would once again take control. The assumption was that they would stay with the same lines and the same strategy that had gotten us into the second round, but Coaches Rizzo and Hendrix had a different idea. (Nature abhors a vacuum.) They pulled Parky, Albert, and me aside. All our kids had made significant contributions in the first round. Coach Rizzo spoke softly, a doctor delivering bad news. He told us that, as well as our kids had played, the team, as presently deployed, stood no chance against the Double As. "They are just too good and just too fast," he said. "What we've been doing will not work. We'll get blown out. So we've made some changes."

The new strategy was clear three minutes into the opening period. Whereas we had been playing three lines, with each line getting equal ice time and contributing to the offense, we were now essentially playing just five kids: Broadway Jenny at center, Tommy at right wing, Joey at left wing, and Brian Rizzo and Barry Meese on defense. This group would skate for two to three minutes, then be relieved by whoever happened to be next up on the bench. That second makeshift grab bag of a line would play for no more than fifty seconds, then make way for the return of the five-player super line. In the course of the game, the first line would play for around thirty minutes. The rest of the team would split the fifteen remaining minutes between them.

Patrick and Duffy argued with the coaches, who told them to sit down and shut up or they would not play at all. Roman and Leo unsnapped their helmets on the bench, a universal sign of surrender. Rick Stanley refused to go on even when his turn did come around. He cursed and was benched for the rest of the game. Many of the parents did not understand what was happening at first. You had to count minutes and look for patterns. When they did understand, they were furious. What's wrong with these parent-coaches? Has the nearness of victory driven them mad? Have they become drunk with ambition? Do they have tournament fever? At times like this, you need a compass to keep your sense of direction, but our leaders had neither compass nor code.

Even major league coaches refuse to do what our parent-coaches had done—remake the roster at the end with a single game in mind, which is a betrayal of the team and the season. Asked to explain his loyalty to his regular pitching rotation in the World Series, the Dodgers manager Tommy Lasorda once said, "You dance with the girl that brung ya." That's the code. Duffy Taylor, our team's leading scorer, was sitting idle at the end of the bench, staring dully ahead. Micah, Leo, Roman, Broadway Julie, Becky, Rick, and Patrick were all doing the same. The hockey gods had tested Coaches Rizzo and Hendrix, and they had failed.

And it wasn't even working. Our skaters, as skilled as some of them were, were gassed by the end of the first period. You simply can't play a single line that much. You need every kid to contribute if you want to compete, a truth clearly known to the Double As, who were rolling three full lines of offense and defense. We were trying to beat fifteen with five. As Coach Hendrix himself might have once said, "It just wasn't good team hockey."

Tommy McDermott scored early—unassisted on a breakaway—but was soon exhausted by our strategy. Like the other forwards, he stopped moving his feet and glided. He stopped back-checking, leaving our overwhelmed defense to fend for itself. For long stretches, we could not get the puck out of our zone. Dan Arcus was characteristically brilliant in goal, but he was like the kid with his finger in the dike. How long could you expect him to hold back the flood? Jocko Arcus was cursing behind the Plexiglas, imploring the coaches to send in fresh skaters.

If we did somehow get the puck out of our zone, Brian Rizzo, urgent to keep the game close, would jump into the offensive rush, try something fancy, and invariably lose the puck, leaving Dan to face the full force of the Double A onslaught alone. Dan was like a target in a shooting gallery, spun this way and that by grapeshot. "Goddamnit," Jocko shouted, banging the glass, "get him some help!"

Halfway through the second, when the score was still relatively close—we were down 3–1—Dan finally broke. You could see it; his shoulders slumped, his stance relaxed. He'd been staring into the maw for twenty minutes. Exhausted and realizing no help was coming, he removed his finger from the dike and let the flood come. By the middle of the third, even easy shots were beating him. The Ridgefield Pee Wee A parents sat silently in the stands as the Ridgefield Double A parents celebrated.

There is a moment near the end of *The Bad News Bears*, the Walter Matthau movie. In the middle of the championship game, when the mood is so tense that it seems the fate of the world is at stake, the camera pulls back. You see other fields with other games, then, beyond that, cars going by on the road, and so remember that none of this really matters, that it's just another game in a game-filled world. That's what we needed at the Whale—a panorama, an establishing shot. We got Jack Camus crying on the bench instead, his mother, Simone, ranting in French. We got Tommy McDermott shouting at Coach Hendrix, imploring him to put other kids into the game. We got Dan Arcus banging his stick on the crossbar after letting in a goal that made the score 9–1. We got Barry Meese passing the puck to the wrong team, and Brian Rizzo turning his back on the play, and Joey McDermott gliding lazily end-to-end. Broadway Jenny being knocked clean off her skates was the last thing we got, which happened as the final horn blew. Everything the coaches had told the kids about hustle and teamwork had been violated in the course of a single afternoon.

There is dignity in losing if you lose as a team, but what could the kids take away from this? What would we tell them on the way home? That life isn't fair? That if you want to play in the big games, make sure your mother runs for the board or your father's a coach? It would be Leo's and Duffy's last season in the program. They'd go on to play on better teams in Greenwich and Stamford, teams Coach Hendrix told them they were not good enough to make. Patrick Campi would make Bantam Double A, while Tommy and Joey McDermott went to Bantam A. Broadway Jenny and Broadway Julie, despite disparity in playing time, ended up on the same roster—Bantam B. Micah moved up to Pee Wee Double A, as did Roman Holian and Brian Rizzo. But all that came later. In the meantime, our kids were going listlessly through the handshake line. They bickered in the locker room. Duffy Taylor denounced the parent-coaches as "F-tards." Roman Holian agreed, then lost it completely. He was not the only player crying.

Coach Rizzo came out to talk to the parents.

He said, "Go in and comfort your kids."

"Why?" asked Sue Campi.

"They're crying," said Coach Rizzo.

"*Why* are they crying?" asked Albert Moriarty.

"They're heartbroken about the loss," said Coach Rizzo.

"Bullshit," said Jerry Sherman. "If they're crying, it's because you humiliated them. What a way to end the season! Play five months as a team, then finish as a single line."

"Yeah, why did you do that?" asked Albert.

"We had to play our best kids if we wanted to compete," said Coach Rizzo.

"We lost eleven to one," said Sue. "How's that competing?"

"It would've been even worse if we'd played your kids," said Coach Rizzo.

The state tournament is usually the end of the season. Due to an odd bit of scheduling, we still had four regular-season games. But the team was never the same. It had split into hostile parties: there were the parents of the five who'd played, then everyone else. These groups would neither talk nor sit together. Albert and Sue refused to go inside the rink at all. They waited outside in their cars during practices and games. Coach Pete, who returned without explanation, tried and failed to heal the rift.

Why did all this bother me? Why did I care so much about the rise and fall of a Pee Wee hockey team? Why did I spend nights on the phone with my father and other fathers, talking and texting? Why did I sleep fitfully or not sleep at all? Why had I come to dread 3:00 a.m., the witching hour, when the clock sounds like a hammer and there is a noise in the kitchen and I'd get lost in a mental loop, in which each move, shot, and game of the season was attempted, taken, and played again? Why was I angry at the parent-coaches? Why was I angry at myself? Why had I become so agitated in the course of the season that I had to remove myself from road trips and rinks altogether?

It was just so hard watching what was done to this team. The Pee Wee As had started as an accidentally beautiful collection of hockey kids. They were fun to watch because they were having fun—passing, goofing, and playing together. Then, over the weeks, sometimes in pursuit of a collective goal, sometimes in pursuit of an individual interest, the parent-coaches remade the team in the image of the grown-up world, breaking its spirit with the weight of their adult needs. But if you asked the kids, they'd tell you that all of it, even the losing, had been fun. Most of them didn't care what line they played on, or for how many minutes, as long as they were treated fairly and with respect, as long as they were part of the team. And they had improved as players, all of them, having sucked every nutrient out of the bitter fruit of defeat.

Parky Taylor, who'd suffered more than the rest of us, said something at the end of March that sounded like wisdom. "From here on," he told me, "I'm going to let Duffy fight these battles himself."

APRIL

T. S. Eliot called April "the cruelest month," but T. S. Eliot was wrong. February is the cruelest month. April is a hand clearing the frost off the window so that you can see the hills. In Ridgefield, it arrives like a green messiah bringing visions of hammocks and white-wine coolers. Afternoons are gentle. You open your eyes to the sound of lawn mowers and the smell of fresh-cut grass.

The joy that animated the Pee Wee A Bears at the start of the season was still there and always had been, only sublimated, buried beneath tirades, drills, and statistics. In those final weeks, after the state tournament, when the algorithm released us from its steely grip, the games were fun again because they were games again, an end in themselves.

As luck had it, the Pee Wee As played their final game against the Pee Wee Double As. A rematch, a do-over. Some of us met for breakfast that morning, our last meal as a team. It made me sad. You spend so much time with these people, more time than you spend with anyone other than the people who live in your house. You form a society and come to think of these other parents as friends. Then, in a moment, it's all over. With tryouts for the next season a few weeks away, these friends become rivals, and once again, it's every man and woman for himself or herself.

Coach Pete, perhaps seeking to right a wrong, went back to the original lines for that final game, with everyone getting equal time. Micah and Duffy played center. Coaches Rizzo and Hendrix welcomed this. Though they did not say so explicitly, they seemed to believe we'd get trounced, proving the correctness of their state-tournament strategy. But that's not what happened. The team, all fifteen of them, having been given an unexpected shot at redemption, played great hockey—hustled, passed, set up goals, and scored. When I looked at the clock, it was the end of the third period and we were winning 5–3. A Double A parent pulled me aside in the lobby after the game and asked why we hadn't played like that at the Whale.

"You could have won it all," he said.

But it didn't matter. All of this was now the past. The sun was shining when we left the rink. It was almost too hot. "I'm sorry it's over," I told Micah.

"Don't be," he said. "We've got baseball."

Acknowledgments

Like hockey, getting a book from inside your head to out in the world is a team effort. I'd like to thank the following teammates (if there is any of this book you hate, that part is their fault): Jonathan Galassi at Farrar, Straus and Giroux; Jennifer Walsh and Jay Mandel at William Morris; Aaron, Nate, Micah, and EZ Cohen—and Jessica!—in Ridgefield; Herb Cohen, Steven Cohen, and Lisa Melmed in Brooklyn; Sharon and Bill Levin on the road between residences; Coach Freeberg at the Deerfield Bubble; and Ellen Eisenstadt Cohen in the Celestial City, where she is drinking a Bloody Mary while being serenaded by Francis Albert Sinatra.